A Practical Guide to

Computer Programming Management

AUERBACH Data Processing Management Library

James Hannan, Editor

•

Contributors To This Volume

George N. Baird
Woodbridge VA

———

Paul F. Barbuto, Jr.
Data Base Manager, Washington State Library Network
Olympia WA

———

Norman Carter
Development Systems International, Los Angeles CA

———

David M. Clark
Computer Applications Consultant, Richmond VA

———

James F. Gross
Sheboygan WI

———

Kathryn Heninger
IBM Corporation, Chapel Hill NC

———

Paul Oliver
President, EDS-World Corporation, Bethesda MD

———

David Schechter
Consultant, Adjunct Assistant Professor of Management
School of Continuing Education, New York University, New York NY

———

John E. Shore
Naval Research Laboratory, Washington DC

———

Bruce Winrow
Wolfe Computer Aptitude Testing Incorporated
Montreal, Canada

———

A Practical Guide to

Computer Programming Management

Edited by James Hannan

AUERBACH Publishers Incorporated
Pennsauken NJ

VAN NOSTRAND REINHOLD COMPANY
New York Cincinnati Toronto London Melbourne

Printed in the United States of America

Published in the United States in 1982
by Van Nostrand Reinhold Company Inc
135 West 50th Street
New York NY 10020 USA

16 15 14 13 12 11 10 9 8 7 6 5 4 3 2 1

Library of Congress Cataloging in Publication Data
Main entry under title:

A Practical guide to computer programming management.

(Auerbach data processing management library ; v. 2)
1. Computer programming management. I. Hannan,
James, 1946-   . II. Series.
QA76.6.P677   1982   658'.054   82-11339
ISBN 0-442-20920-7 (Van Nostrand Reinhold Co. : pbk.)

Contents

Preface

In its relatively brief existence, the computer has emerged from the back rooms of most organizations to become an integral part of business life. Increasingly sophisticated data processing systems are being used today to solve increasingly complex business problems. As a result, the typical data processing function has become as intricate and specialized as the business enterprise it serves.

Such specialization places a strenuous burden on computer professionals. Not only must they possess specific technical expertise, they must understand how to apply their special knowledge in support of business objectives and goals. A computer professional's effectiveness and career hinge on how ably he or she manages this challenge.

To assist computer professionals in meeting this challenge, AUERBACH Publishers has developed the *AUERBACH Data Processing Management Library*. The series comprises eight volumes, each addressing the management of a specific DP function:

A Practical Guide to Data Processing Management
A Practical Guide to Programming Management
A Practical Guide to Data Communications Management
A Practical Guide to Data Base Management
A Practical Guide to Systems Development Management
A Practical Guide to Data Center Operations Management
A Practical Guide to EDP Auditing
A Practical Guide to Distributed Processing Management

Each volume contains well-tested, practical solutions to the most common and pressing set of problems facing the manager of that function. Supplying the solutions is a prominent group of DP practitioners—people who make their living in the areas they write about. The concise, focused chapters are designed to help the reader directly apply the solutions they contain to his or her environment.

AUERBACH has been serving the information needs of computer professionals for more than 25 years and knows how to help them increase their effectiveness and enhance their careers. The *AUERBACH Data Processing Management Library* is just one of the company's many offerings in this field.

James Hannan
Assistant Vice President
AUERBACH Publishers

Introduction

Perhaps no other function in data processing has gained the notoriety that programming has. To the uninitiated, it is the most impenetrable of all the DP black arts, with technical sorcerers employing ritualistic "methodologies" and arcane "languages" to make the electronic leviathan do their bidding. Solutions to the most complex business and scientific problems can be had simply by petitioning the sorcerers, who then produce results in the time it takes to utter the requisite incantations.

For most programming managers, this naive but all-too-prevalent attitude on the part of users is a fact they must cope with in meeting their organizations' need for application systems. Creating programs entails the skillful management of both people and technology, a process that many managers might argue is almost as difficult as conjuring spells. And whether users are knowledgeable or uninformed about the realities of programming, they generally make rigorous demands of programming managers. This volume of the *AUERBACH Data Processing Management Library* is designed to help programming managers satisfy those demands.

We have commissioned an outstanding group of DP practitioners to share the benefits of their extensive and varied experience in programming. Our authors have written on a carefully chosen range of topics and have provided proven, practical advice for managing the programming function more efficiently and effectively.

In Chapter One, Bruce Winrow discusses an effective way to deal with the chronic shortage of experienced programmers—hiring and training entry-level programmers. He provides guidelines for hiring high-potential graduates from educational institutions and outlines procedures for establishing an entry-level training program.

In addition to hiring and training programmers, a manager is also responsible for assessing programmer performance. Such assessments help reduce turnover by keeping programmers informed about their strengths, weaknesses, and progress. In his "Performance Appraisal of Programmers," Norman Carter discusses techniques that help managers make and understand evaluations; he also offers procedures, a checklist, and sample forms that can facilitate performance appraisal.

As challenging as personnel issues are, the programming manager must also deal with an equally demanding set of technical problems. Determining the resources required to develop a software product is one such problem. In Chapter Three, Paul Oliver explains why it is so difficult to develop accurate estimates and suggests policies, procedures, and formats that can reduce the level of difficulty and improve the accuracy of estimates.

Introduction

System design is another subject that presents knotty technical problems. Managers and programmers are often encouraged to design modular programs to increase software reliability and reduce overall software costs. Kathryn Heninger and John E. Shore introduce the basic concepts of modular program design and explain how to apply them in Chapter Four.

In the area of program design, an effective but often overlooked technique is the use of decision tables. Most programming tools are valuable at a specific stage in the program life cycle but do not serve nearly as well at other stages. Decision tables, on the other hand, can be used with equal effect in analysis, design, programming, and documentation. In Chapter Five, Paul F. Barbuto, Jr., discusses the construction, modification, and uses of decision tables.

Since many programs are moved from computer to computer during their lifetimes, it makes economic sense to consider the costs of portability at the design stage. In "Program Portability," Paul Oliver describes the problems inherent in portability and discusses how to minimize software conversion costs during program design and implementation.

Many of the problems and costs associated with program design and implementation can be reduced or eliminated through the development and enforcement of standard policies and procedures. In "Writing Straightforward, Maintainable Programs," James F. Gross examines some of the factors that make programs hard to maintain and suggests some general considerations and specific coding practices that can yield more maintainable programs. George N. Baird presents guidelines for producing source programs that appear as though written by a single programmer, thus facilitating maintenance, in his "Programming Style in COBOL." And David Schechter describes a technique for reducing implementation costs in his chapter detailing the skeleton program approach to implementation.

The testing phase of program development can benefit as much from the use of top-down methods as the design phase. Moving the testing process forward in the development cycle and integrating it into top-down design enables testing to provide timely feedback. Paul Barbuto describes top-down testing and the tools that support it in Chapter Ten.

Although it consumes a significant amount of time and resources, program maintenance is generally viewed as an uncontrollable necessity. To help bring this activity under control, David M. Clark presents a workable methodology for program maintenance that emphasizes programmer preparation, program and task overviews, and change follow-through.

1 Acquiring Entry-Level Programmers
by Bruce Winrow

INTRODUCTION

Many organizations are encountering difficulties caused by the severe shortage of experienced programmers. The various recruiting alternatives are expensive and often unfruitful. In addition, even experienced personnel often require considerable training to become familiar with an organization's unique mix of hardware, software packages, programming techniques, project methodologies, and so on.

As a result, an increasing number of programming managers are establishing entry-level training courses to attract high-potential (but inexperienced) graduates of educational institutions. The aim is to produce—as quickly as possible—productive programmers trained to meet the organization's specific needs. Recent graduates can be hired at lower salaries than experienced programmers. Hiring inexperienced candidates also encourages promotion from within for other job openings, and effective programmer training can reduce turnover.

In this chapter, it is assumed that the reader is familiar with the basic tasks involved in undertaking a training needs analysis, exploring training sources, and setting up the training program. This chapter discusses the need for management commitment to entry-level training and recruiting, the value of aptitude testing for entry-level candidates, and a proven procedure for hiring trainees. A case study of a large DP installation is presented.

MANAGEMENT COMMITMENT

Senior management support is essential for success in hiring programmer trainees. This support will come only after an appropriate presentation that outlines the cost and benefits of setting up a training program and recruiting entry-level personnel. Approval must be obtained for the anticipated hiring costs, the training budget, and the salary scale for the new trainees. There are several advantages in hiring trainees in groups; therefore, senior management should be encouraged to identify manpower requirements for the coming year or two.

ROLE OF THE TRAINING DEPARTMENT

If the organization includes a training department, this department must establish its role in the hiring process, and senior management must demonstrate its support of that role. Often, department managers or personnel departments hire new employees and turn them over to the training department to upgrade their skills. The problem with this procedure is that different managers use different criteria for selection and have varying degrees of skill in the hiring process (e.g., interviewing). Even though the training department often has to train less-than-ideal candidates, the trainers are still held responsible for the new employee's performance. If the training department is judged by the performance of its trainees, it behooves the training manager to have some control over the quality of the candidates.

Many organizations, of course, have no separate training department; consequently, essential functions of establishing the program, obtaining management support, determining hiring criteria, and coordinating the efforts must be performed by other appropriate personnel. The trainers can be drawn from programming managers, senior programmers, personnel department staff, and so on.

RECRUITING PROGRAMMER TRAINEES

Hiring high-aptitude candidates maximizes the likelihood of success. Hiring poor candidates, even at the entry level, is expensive and can be disastrous. Selection techniques are limited and usually involve screening résumés, interviewing, checking references, and objective testing. To use only one of these approaches would be irresponsible, especially since all but testing are more or less subjective.

As with any other worthwhile project, the most important step in the recruiting process is planning. Figure 1-1 illustrates a network plan for hiring entry-level trainees. This plan has proved successful for a large organization with approximately 2,500 DP employees at all skill levels.

It is essential to identify the type of individual desired, where he or she can be found, and the best recruiting method. Four obvious groups that may provide candidates for entry-level programming positions are:
- University graduates whose curricula include DP courses
- Community college graduates in DP
- Graduates of an accredited computer institute
- Internal candidates possessing a high aptitude for programming

If the organization plans to put the new workers through a comprehensive training program, the recruiting process need not be limited to computer science graduates. The greater the candidates' exposure to such courses, however, the greater the chance they will know what they are getting into, and the less chance they will resign because they "just don't like data processing." Some exposure to DP may also make the training process easier.

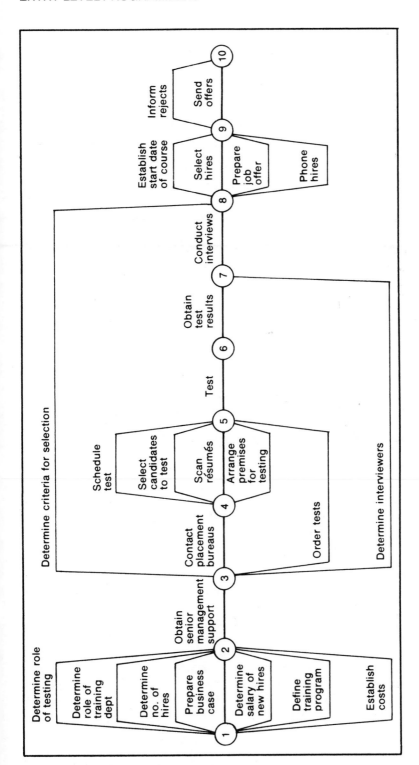

Figure 1-1. Sample Network Plan for Hiring Programmer Trainees

Many educational institutions have a placement service that will supply organizations with résumés of graduating students on request. At the very least, notices can be posted on campus, announcing the organization's intent to hire. The training manager should survey local schools to determine which offer courses that best match the organization's needs. Advertising in local papers and using placement agencies are other alternatives, but these can be time consuming and very expensive, especially for entry-level personnel.

Prior to obtaining résumés, the criteria for screening should be determined. Some criteria (e.g., scholastic average, work experience, curriculum) may have particular value to an employer. The job requirements should be studied (even for entry-level personnel) in order to compare the candidate's qualifications with the needs of the job. The résumés should then be read over carefully, noting such things as gaps in background, inconsistencies, insufficient information, reasons for leaving previous employment, and attitudes.

If testing is used as a tool for selection, administrative details must be taken care of first. This may include arranging for testing premises and ensuring that there are enough tests on hand. Potential employees will be taking the test, and the company should give a professional first impression. There is no excuse for administrative foul-ups, considering the enormous value of hiring the best candidates. As many candidates as possible should be tested at one sitting, especially if many of them are being recruited from the same educational institution. Avoid using the same test more than once for students from a single institution. Some applicants who have already spent hundreds of dollars on programming courses may rationalize that there is nothing wrong with getting "help" with the test as long as they finally understand how to do the problems. Most good tests are designed on the assumption that the problems are new to the applicant. Scheduling as few testing sessions as possible greatly reduces the problem of one applicant coaching another.

APTITUDE TESTING AND HIRING DISCRIMINATION

Because of the intense EEOC scrutiny to which aptitude tests have been subjected, many employers wonder whether they are allowed by law to use objective tests as part of their selection criteria. Employers should realize that testing is not illegal; it is not even disapproved of. Organizations are free to use any professionally developed aptitude test that is not discriminatory. They are also free to use a test that, in practice, screens out protected classes of individuals in disproportionate numbers, provided the test can be shown to be a valid indicator of on-the-job performance.

Both public and private employers with 15 or more employees who work at least 20 weeks per year must comply with EEOC guidelines. The guidelines cover any procedure used to make an employment decision, including interviewing, reviewing applications and work experience, oral and written tests, physical requirements, and so on. The fundamental principle of the guidelines is that employer policies or practices having adverse impact—as determined by the "4/5 rule" illustrated in Table 1-1—on the employment opportunities of

Table 1-1. Determination of Adverse Impact (4/5 Rule)

Selection Procedure Administered to	Hired	Percentage Selected	Hiring Ratio*
100 males	65 males	65	
60 females	20 females	33	33/65 (50%)

*In this example, the hiring ratio for females is less than 80% of that for males, indicating hiring practices adversely affect females. This means the selection procedure must be validated.

---

any race, sex, or ethnic group are not permissable unless justified by business necessity.

Employers who use a selection procedure that has no adverse affect on a protected group may avoid application of the guidelines. Selection procedures that do have adverse impact should be validated to demonstrate the relationship between the procedure and on-the-job performance. In the case of testing, scores must be predictive of performance on the job. If the employer has substantial evidence of the validity of a particular test, it may be used in the selection procedure while data is collected for a local validation study. To determine ''substantial evidence,'' the abilities required for successful performance of the jobs should be established, and these criteria should be compared to what is measured by the test. If the criteria in the job description and those in the test are very much the same, and if the test has been validated elsewhere, the test can be used. It should be considered only one factor (less than 50 percent) in making the selection decision.

To perform a validation study, a sample of at least 30 persons—either present employees (concurrent validation) or new hires (predictive validation)—must be measured over a period of time to determine whether there is a meaningful relationship (predictive validation coefficient) between on-the-job performance ratings and the test predictions. The testing/test marketing organization should gather the data on the employer's behalf, perform all necessary statistical work, and provide a detailed written validation report showing the results of the study for the employer's organization.

At least three factors should be considered when selecting a test to use:
- Relevance—A relevant test measures abilities that are critical to job success.
- Reliability—A reliable test should predict success on the job over a long period of time and with a wide range of applications.
- Predicting on-the-job success—There should be close agreement of test scores and supervisory ratings of performance on the job.

To optimize fairness, time-limited and multiple-choice tests should be avoided. In addition, physical security measures during the test-taking procedure should be considered to ensure against cheating. When evaluating cost, a better test should not be discounted just because it is more expensive: the higher cost is justified if the test prevents hiring a poor candidate.

THE INTERVIEW PROCESS

Screening résumés and testing are only two tools in the selection procedure and, although they are important, they involve very little interaction between the organization and the candidate. The interview process, if well planned and executed, can mean the difference between hiring excellent candidates and not meeting the recruiting quota.

First, qualified interviewers should be chosen, and the same interviewers should be used throughout the hiring campaign. If experienced interviewers are not available, a course on effective interviewing should be considered.

In one successful organization, the training manager, an employment coordinator from the personnel department, and the programmer training instructor separately interview each candidate. After all candidates have been seen, each interviewer arranges the applicants in order of preference. A general meeting takes place to merge the lists and select those to whom job offers will be sent.

The interviewers should meet before the interviews and plan their approach. They should establish objectives for interviewing and, as much as possible, avoid duplication of questions or areas of discussion. Planning also facilitates probing for in-depth information; inexperienced interviewers often try to cover too many items in too short a time and might never, for example, uncover the real reason for a job change.

Careful scheduling is also important. Applicants appreciate professionalism and are impressed when they are interviewed on time by three successive people, with no delays in between. This can be accomplished by allowing each interviewer about 45 minutes (30 minutes for the interview and 15 minutes to document the evaluation). At the end of 30 minutes, the candidate is brought to the next interviewer. Each interviewer must be well prepared and familiar with the applicant's résumés. With this system, the candidate is finished with three interviews in 90 minutes, with no delays (this assumes that the interviewers are in close proximity).

Another benefit of planning the interview procedure is establishing the "selling approach." The demand for high-potential programming graduates is increasing as more and more organizations establish training programs and hire entry-level people. Once an organization finds a person who fits the job opening, there remains the task of convincing the candidate to pick that organization above several others. In many organizations, this aspect of the interview process is neglected or handled very poorly. A hard-sell approach is frequently not appreciated by applicants; however, an experienced interviewer who is enthusiastic about his or her company and can incorporate the likes and dislikes mentioned by the applicants into the discussion is a very valuable asset. The interviewer should capitalize on the benefits the organization offers and provide direct answers to inquiries about the functions the applicant would perform and the career paths available. The more specific and honest an interviewer can be, the greater the likelihood that the desired programmers will be hired and retained.

It is important that the organization remain in constant contact with the applicant at all stages of the selection process. This reduces the chances of surprise if a candidate accepts a position elsewhere; in addition, it improves the organization's professional image. Every applicant, whether accepted or rejected, should receive some sort of response. The vehicle may be a form letter or a personal phone call. A company with good follow-up procedures has a competitive edge over those with shoddy hiring practices. Even though a candidate is turned down, he or she may be in a position to refer future candidates; thus, the interview process should leave all candidates with a positive image of the organization.

THE JOB OFFER

Before making a job offer (even, in fact, before initiating the interview process), competitive salary ranges for entry-level programmers should be established. Many companies set their pay scales according to scholastic attainment and thus offer salaries that depend on whether the applicant is a community college, computer institute, or university graduate. It is possible to offer lower than competitive salaries if there is an extensive entry-level training program; however, the salaries should be made competitive at the end of training, or the students who have completed the program may be enticed to other firms.

Consideration should be given to raising everyone's salary to the same level at the completion of training, regardless of educational background. If the training is effective, the students will have similar abilities to perform similar jobs. Salary figures that competent performers can expect after training and after one year with the organization should be identified. Commitment to these figures when making a job offer can help offset any negative feelings an applicant might have about a less-than-competitive starting salary.

It is important to be careful about having the applicant sign a contract committing him or her to the firm for a period of time in an attempt to guarantee some return for the training. If the individual becomes disgruntled, the firm may be better off without him or her.

Before writing the job offer, it is wise to inform the applicant by telephone that it is coming. This may cause the applicant to stop job hunting; it also provides an opportunity for the applicant to affirm his or her interest in the position.

CASE STUDY OF A LARGE DP INSTALLATION

The procedure outlined in Figure 1-1 has been used for eight years by a very large bank that hires approximately 40 programmer trainees every year. The bank conducts four training sessions a year, with approximately 10 students in each session. The course begins on the date of hire and lasts for 20 weeks. Aptitude testing is used extensively both for selection and for identifying possible "fast trackers." A recent study conducted by the bank revealed that employees who were hired when testing was part of the selection procedure were rated higher—by a margin of approximately 20 percent—by their managers than candidates selected without testing.

The bank's training department was responsible for both recruiting and training the new personnel. Table 1-2 indicates the cost of hiring 10 candidates and training them in a five-month course.

Table 1-2. Budget for Hiring and Training 10 Trainees

		$1,000
Management Salaries (0.8 man-years)		21
Clerical		4
Trainee Salaries		50
	Subtotal	75
Aptitude Tests		3
Training Materials*		4
Computer Time		12
Hardware (TSO terminal rental)		5
Premises		11
Travel		1
	Total	111
	Cost/Trainee	11.1
	Cost/Trainee/Month	2.2

*This amount represents replacement costs only, since this organization owns most of its training materials.

The bank found that graduates of the training program performed at a level comparable to that of an externally hired programmer with approximately two years of experience. Part of the cost justification for the training was that the five-month graduates, who were familiarized with organization-specific procedures and became productive quickly, were paid a lower salary than their counterparts with two years of experience. In addition, turnover was lower, in part because entry-level personnel are not attractive to other firms until they gain some experience. Over an eight-year period, the average yearly turnover rate of personnel who had completed the training (approximately 350 people) was 8.8 percent. Those who did resign stayed for an average of 2.6 years.

The bank used the scale in Table 1-3 for entry-level salaries. As can be seen, all students were brought to the same salary level towards the end of the training program and were reviewed again in six months. It was felt that the 10-month review was necessary for competitive reasons, especially since the graduates were by then fully productive. From that point, the bank's yearly salary policy took over, with employees receiving a five to ten percent increase based on performance ratings established by the employee's immediate supervisor. In addition, the bank usually granted a six to nine percent across-the-board increase (a market adjustment for competent or better-than-competent employees).

The benefit of determining this salary scale in advance was that the 10-month salary of $15,700 could be quoted in the job offer, and it appeared more

Table 1-3. Salary Scale for Entry-Level Programmers

Time	Education	Salary
Entry	1-year institute	$11,200
	2-year community college	11,760
	University	12,400
4 months	Everyone	13,800
10 months	Everyone	15,700
22 months	Everyone	5–10% merit
		6–9% market

competitive than the entry-level rates. The interviewers explained the training program to the applicants to ensure that they understood why the initial salary was low. Using this procedure, the bank had no difficulty in attracting and keeping good candidates.

The bank experienced another benefit from hiring and training in groups. With several people going through the same curriculum, students with performance problems were identified and dealt with early. (In some instances this meant dismissal.) This relieved individual supervisors of the burden of identifying poor performers, provided a more objective means of evaluation, and saved the company time and money by releasing substandard personnel before they became long-term employees.

During the 20-week training program, the training manager received requests from other managers for the services of the graduating students. The training manager, knowing the capabilities of the students and the work requirements of the various requesting areas, made a preliminary allocation of students to the various managers. Interviews were arranged, and if the manager and student reached a mutual agreement, the graduating student was assigned a position. If there were problems (such as personality clashes), other interviews were held until good matches could be found. Because of careful manpower planning, in eight years there were never more graduating students than available positions at the end of training.

CONCLUSION

When hiring entry-level programmers for a training program, the following points should be considered:
- Plan the recruiting process, and adopt a uniform recruiting procedure.
- Obtain budget approval in advance for recruiting and training.
- Use selection tools wherever possible in the hiring process.
- Hire candidates for their potential, and train them in the necessary skills.
- Consider long-term manpower requirements, and hire and train in groups.
- Determine the role the training department should take in the recruiting process.
- Establish an entry-level salary scale and subsequent salary progression for the new trainees.

- Conduct planned and professional interviews with appropriate follow-up.
- Identify standards of performance for the training program so that substandard trainees can be identified early.

Following these guidelines can help staff the organization with productive, satisfied programmers.

2 Performance Appraisal of Programmers

by Norman Carter

INTRODUCTION

DP employees with excellent working tools (e.g., systems development methodologies and test data generators) are usually well trained in their use. The question of how well the individual actually uses these tools, however, is often ignored. Some managers apparently feel that a raise and an occasional pat on the back obviate the need for formal employee evaluation.

Companies that conduct regular feedback interviews six months after employees leave have found that lack of effective performance appraisal is high on the list of reasons for leaving. In many cases, this reason precedes the financial motivation so often discussed at the time of leaving. If lack of effective performance appraisal is indeed a major reason for employee turnover, there are straightforward ways to attack the problem.

There is another reason for conducting regular formal performance appraisal of DP personnel: both the Equal Employment Opportunity Commission (EEOC) and Affirmative Action (AA) require that a company be able to demonstrate a direct and traceable relationship among a job description, performance criteria for the job, appraisal of performance against the description and criteria, and direct involvement of the individual in setting, monitoring, and measuring objectives.

Objectives of Performance Appraisal

The primary objectives of performance appraisal are to:
- Review employee progress in terms directly related to the organization and the individual's job family and position
- Review and establish measurable performance goals for the next given time period
- Design objectives, action plans, and training curricula for each individual for current, and in preparation for future, job responsibilities
- Comply with company personnel and salary administration policies and guidelines

Justification for a requested salary increase is not among these objectives. In fact, a combined performance and compensation appraisal detracts from the objectivity of the performance evaluation; the manager may find that in order to support a requested increase, he must make unsupported statements or statements that do not reflect a consistent view of the individual's contribution to the department.

Performance appraisal provides the framework within which the growth of an employee can be evaluated independently of the availability of money to compensate that individual. In fact, consistent appraisals are one lever a manager can use to correct salary grades or ranges with the compensation manager. Once-a-year fudged performance appraisals make correction of salary inequities almost impossible.

Performance appraisal can also be used for mutual discussion of the professional and technical achievements of the employee. Performance objectives can be negotiated, thus avoiding unilateral goal-setting by the manager.

Managers as Coaches, Not Umpires

The role of a manager can be likened to that of the coach of a team. Each player is taught what to do and how to do it in normal circumstances. As the game proceeds, minor adjustments are made by the coach. A coach who does not modify the game plan in response to the play is usually neither respected by his players nor successful in developing or maintaining a winning team.

At the same time, a player has the responsibility to call time-out to discuss a situation he has observed on the field so that the coach can offer further assistance. In this sense, the success of the team is as important as the success of each individual.

Performance appraisal involves the manager, supervisor, or team leader in the coaching or counseling of employees in terms of their ongoing overall development, not just as an umpire dealing with disputes and disruptions. In addition, performance appraisal helps the leader and staff feel like members of a team and helps allay the feeling that each approach by the manager is related to disciplinary action or financial reward.

TYPES OF PERFORMANCE APPRAISAL

Performance appraisal is typically viewed as a single activity: sit down, fill out the form, conduct a cursory everything-is-all-right discussion, sign the form, and get back to work. It is not, however, as simple as that.

Employees generally fall into three categories:
- High performers with high potential
- Average performers
- Marginal performers

Figure 2-1 shows the performance/training activities prescribed for each type of employee. Figure 2-2 shows career planning relationships. These activities and relationships should be considered when preparing employee performance objectives.

Training Activity \ Performance Category	High Performer		Average Performer		Marginal Performer	
	Ready	Future	Short Plan	Long Plan	Keep	Separate
Self-development	High	High	Above average	Average	Low	None expected
Classes/ workshops/ seminars	To round out knowledge	Key subjects for next position	Next required missing skills	Selective skill for advancement	To maintain skill	–
Coaching/counseling	Intensive	Intensive	To supplement skills	To prepare for advancement	To maintain skill	To maintain minimum skill until separation
Involvement in other company activities	High	High	Some	As available	Minimum	–

Figure 2-1. Performance/Training Activity Requirements

The high performer should, of course, be expected to do more than the low performer and should also be expected to perform more job-related development activities outside of work. A low performer, however, who will be separated from the company, may be on the job for longer than expected while a replacement is found. Training may be required to ensure that job skills do not fall below an acceptable level. No other training activities should be scheduled for this category.

Performance Appraisal Roles

Three complementary roles in performance appraisal—the company, the manager, and the individual—can, when linked, provide an effective performance-oriented environment. Effective communication among the three areas is essential.

The three roles can be defined as follows:
- The Company
  - —Provides the overall climate for individual growth
  - —Demands high performance standards
  - —Expects managers to develop their subordinates
  - —Recognizes the need for training and makes it available
  - —Rewards accomplishments financially and in terms of advancement
- The Manager
  - —Provides continuous coaching and guidance
  - —Demands the demonstration of immediate and sustained performance improvement in each assigned task
  - —Expects help from staff resources in the coaching role and recognition for the accomplishment of this role
- The Individual
  - —Is self-motivated in the area of personal and professional growth
  - —Demands a say in determining his or her career path
  - —Expects help from the company and immediate supervisor
  - —Recognizes responsibility for applying his or her training
  - —Rewards the company with an immediate return on investment through increased productivity

A self-assessment guide can also be provided by the company for employee use; no supervisory input is required unless requested by the individual.

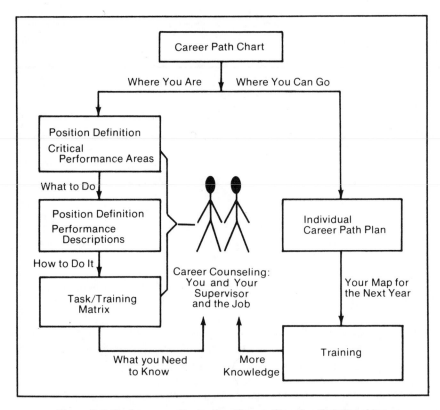

Figure 2-2. Performance Evaluation/Career Planning Relationships

PREPARING FOR THE PERFORMANCE APPRAISAL

As one of the most demanding, difficult, and rewarding managerial activities, effective performance appraisal takes time—and managers often say they have no time for such appraisals. Time can always be found, however, to interview applicants, to correct work if employee objectives have been poorly set, or to provide training when lack of knowledge causes errors. In many cases, more time is required to correct a performance problem than is necessary to conduct an appraisal, set objectives, and help the employee understand them. Preparing and conducting a thorough, effective performance appraisal should require less than five hours per person.

Review and Evaluation of Performance. This step involves gathering the tools for appraisal, reviewing objectives and accomplishments, considering why things were or were not done as agreed, reviewing the employee's overall performance and comparing it with others as appropriate, and identifying training strengths and deficiencies. This crucial preparation activity takes between one and one-and-one-half hours per person.

Discussion. After preparation by the employee and the supervisor, performance, productivity, and new and continuing objectives should be discussed. This step should also take an hour to an hour and a half per person.

Negotiation. If performance evaluation is done consistently and at logical checkpoints throughout the year, differences of opinion and viewpoint should be minimal. Several discussions may be necessary, however, to reach a mutually agreeable set of performance objectives. These discussions may require two meetings of about an hour each.

Completion. Completing and submitting all paperwork in accordance with company procedures (after appraising and ranking all individuals in a section or department) should take about 15 minutes per person.

The Tools

The following types of tools facilitate performance appraisal.

Standard Forms and Procedures. If standard forms and procedures have not been specified by the company, they should be developed and used consistently. This requirement becomes increasingly important as EEOC and AA continue to expand their roles as protectors of employee rights. Standardization also helps avoid government audits that often occur when individuals feel that varying standards are being applied.

Position Descriptions. Job descriptions should be written in specific terms detailing what is to be done and how, in addition to giving broad statements of responsibility and authority.

Job Standards. Job standards and tools should describe project requirements, system development standards and guidelines, departmental standards and policies, and pertinent company policies and procedures.

Assignments/Results. The objectives set for the period should be available for review, as should a list of assignments that may have facilitated or impeded achievement of the objectives.

Previous Appraisals. Several prior appraisals should be available for review to help detect such trends as failure to meet objectives or exceeding objectives frequently.

Setting the Meeting Date

To ensure that both parties are effectively prepared, the employee should receive copies of the performance evaluation forms and instructions at least a week before the discussion date. If special or additional goals have been included, they should be reviewed and communicated to the individual at this time (preferably in writing). Self-assessment aids can also be made available at this time for the individual to use, if desired.

THE PERFORMANCE APPRAISAL DISCUSSION

At best, performance appraisal begins as a stressful interview. Both participants come with different expectations. Until it is understood that the differences are professional and not personal, that compromise need not be one-sided, and that effective negotiation is a sign of professional maturity, the discussion will achieve less than optimum results. The following suggestions help reduce the threatening aspects of the discussion.

The Environment. Do not conduct the discussion in a noisy environment or with other people present. For example, do not hold the meeting in a restaurant where customers and serving make communication difficult. (In addition, it is extremely difficult to enjoy a meal under the constraints of such a critical activity as performance appraisal.)

The best setting is a neutral environment such as a conference room, where both parties can come from behind their desks. In addition, try to ensure that the discussion is not interrupted; in no case should telephone calls be taken by either person during the discussion. Behaviorists state that each time a discussion is interrupted, it takes from five to ten minutes to regain the concentration and flow that existed before the interruption.

The atmosphere should be as comfortable as possible. If the atmosphere of the department is shirt sleeve, keep it that way. Do not set up artificially formal barriers. Have some liquid refreshment (coffee, soft drink, or water) available.

The Discussion. The process must be a discussion, not a monologue. Both parties, but especially the manager, should practice active listening techniques. Notes should be taken and, whenever necessary, read back so that both parties understand and agree on what has been discussed.

Negotiating. When differences of opinion on performance arise, the manager should be prepared to use conflict-resolution skills. Resolutions must be within the scope of and consistent with the performance appraisal tools mentioned earlier. Agreements reached outside these constraints, unless carefully documented and well understood, often lead to additional conflict. They are, therefore, self-defeating as a means of improving performance.

Legal Requirements

Although all of the EEOC rulings and AA requirements cannot be detailed in this chapter, the following points should not be overlooked:
- Compliance with the law is compulsory, not voluntary.
- Intent to follow the law is not sufficient.
- Documentation of appropriate procedures and policies is required in case of audit.

- The responsible organizations have stated that audits of compliance will be conducted more frequently than in the past.

Goal Setting

Two types of goal setting are required for performance evaluations: qualitative and quantitative.

Qualitative Goals. Too often, all of the established goals are qualitative and include such statements as:
- Will maintain a level of production consistent with the average achieved by the group
- Will comply with procedures established by management

Although some qualitative goals can be beneficial, they should be expressed in concrete terms so that the individual understands exactly what is expected. For example, a more explicit qualitative goal might be:
- To comply with the requirements described in the Systems Standards Manual for the appropriate phase of the assigned development tasks
- To comply with Documentation Standard X
- To understand and be guided by Company Policy Y related to attendance on the job

Qualitative goals should be kept to the minimum consistent with the assumption that the employee knows the general requirements of the company and the job.

Quantitative Goals. As far as possible, performance goals should be quantitative and restricted to an attainable number, generally between three and five. With more than five goals, activity and accomplishment tend to become too diffuse, and judgment can become imprecise. Spreading fewer than three goals over a similar period of time tends to make recalling sufficient detail difficult.

A quantitative goal should at least include the following elements:
- A description of the task to be done
- A definition of the standard to be used
- A breakdown of the task into deliverable items and the standard for each
- The relationship of each deliverable to a phase or project activity with earliest/latest completion schedules, such as:

  To complete program A in System B with fewer than three assemblies, using Test Assembly Standard E and Document Standard F. To be completed not later than Date H. Performance of this goal contingent on input from prior program delivery by Date G.

- Statement of the value to the individual in meeting the goal. For example:

  This objective will carry a weight of 50 percent in the next appraisal, based on completion within the schedules established.

JUDGING REWARDS AND PENALTIES

An effective challenge to individuals to improve their performance requires rewards and penalties. Often, the reward is more money and the penalty less, with a range of three to six percent. In view of today's economy, this may not be sufficient motivation. Rewards that are not exclusively tied to money should be used.

Weighted Performance Goals. Once agreed-upon objectives are accepted as the normal, expected performance, the effect of other-than-normal performance can be judged. Weighted goals, which define other-than-standard performance, can be expressed as follows:

- The objective is to complete the tasks on the schedule described and within a budget of $X, over which you have control. Upon completion, your performance reward will be:
  —On schedule, below budget = Normal increase + 10 percent of budget saved
  —Before schedule, below budget = Normal increase + 25 percent of budget saved
  —After schedule or over budget = No increase
- The objective is to successfully implement the XYZ software package in accordance with the vendor's contract terms and planned schedule and to achieve a level of user satisfaction so that fewer than four complaints will be received by senior management in the first three months of operation.
  —Should this occur, 50 percent of your performance award will be earned.
  —If the schedule is missed by more than one month or if user complaints exceed four during that period, the performance award will be decreased to 35 percent.
  —If the schedule is missed by more than three months or if complaints exceed 10, the goal will be considered not met.

These examples show that while weighted goals expedite quantification of rewards, they require considerable thought, precise definition, and tough-mindedness in their enforcement. In most cases, however, a demanding atmosphere, coupled with fair and firm goal-setting and evaluation, is beneficial to the individual and the company.

Additional Techniques

Three additional techniques can be used to make performance appraisal more effective. *Totem poling*, *tie breaking*, and *ranking* aid in weighing individuals against one another; they are perhaps most beneficial in situations where resources and opportunities are limited.

Totem Poling. Totem poling is the listing of all employees in order of performance, top to bottom. The totem pole is constructed from the supervisor's empirical judgment and then refined by the performance appraisals.

Individual Rating	Value Rating

1. Demonstrated ability to bring projects in on time and within budget (±5%)

   3 Usually better   2 As planned   1 Usually misses   x 3

2. Adherence to SDLC Process, stated guidelines, project (Job Procedure)

   3 Always   2 Satisfactory   1 Fails to Comply   x 1

3. Effective user relationships (does not require manager intervention)

   3 Fewer than 2 complaints/yr   2 3 to 5 complaints
   1 More than 6 complaints   x 3

4. Quality Production

   3 Consistently above standard   2 Meets standard
   1 Below standard   x 2

5. Quantity Production

   3 Consistently above standard   2 Meets standard
   1 Below standard   x 2

6. Meeting agreed-upon objectives

   3 Usually betters performance   2 Meets at least 2 out of 3
   1 Rarely meets   x 1

7. Making creative input outside of assigned project area

   3 Often (2 to 3 times/yr)   2 Sometimes (1/yr)   1 Rarely x 1

8. Applies training received, when back on job

   3 Always   2 Sometimes   1 Rarely   x 1

9. Consistency and accuracy of project planning and estimating

   3 Plan always met (barring outside intervention)   2 Plan met
   80% of time   1 Plan met less than half the time   x 3

10. Knows and actively supports management objectives

    3 Always   2 Usually   1 Rarely   x 2

Figure 2-3. Typical Tie-Breaking Questions

Inconsistencies in judgment at appraisal time are minimized since the person completing the totem pole is forced to ask:

Why have I put this person in this place? Is this placement consistent with the performance appraisal rating?

Tie Breaking. Some form of tie breaking is required when two or more employees seem to have identical ratings but only one can be selected for advancement. Pertinent rating questions can be developed, with the value of each determined on a basis acceptable to all managers involved in the selection process. Figure 2-3 shows the kinds of questions and value rating that can be created.

With this tie-breaking technique, each individual is rated and the score calculated by multiplying the numeric value of the answer by the value rating and adding all rated items. The result can be used as one input to help break a tie.

Ranking. Totem poles of the employees in an organization (or department) can be combined for similar job families or project groups. This provides top-to-bottom ranking of all programmers, for example, covered by one job description. Using a master ranking list, management can:

- Identify evaluation inconsistencies between organizations or supervisors
- Identify candidates
  —For advancement
  —For evaluation of low performance
  —Who are expected to change ranking position during the next 12 to 24 months

PERFORMANCE APPRAISAL PROCEDURES

Regularly conducted performance appraisals are vital in keeping programmers aware of how well they are doing in their jobs. Use of standard forms and procedures makes the performance appraisal process easier to accomplish and to apply consistently. This enables managers and employees to communicate more freely; it also helps meet EEOC and AA requirements. The remainder of this chapter describes standardized procedures for planning, preparing, and conducting performance evaluations and shows the types of forms that can be used.

STEPS IN PERFORMANCE EVALUATION

The steps to be taken in conducting an effective appraisal, including preparation, the discussion itself, and follow-through, are indicated in subsequent sections.

Planning Procedures

- Review with the employee the position description, task definition, job standards or requirements, and other pertinent procedures or policy statements.
- Establish personal objectives. Briefly discuss performance evaluation and career planning as it relates to company policy.

During the Year

- Give ongoing feedback to the employee about his or her strengths and weaknesses.
- Solicit the individual's input on how well he or she is accomplishing the set objectives. Adjust goals as needed.
- Monitor performance, and keep notes. Perform interim evaluations as goals are reached or as observation indicates a necessity for corrective action or review.

Before the Formal Appraisal

- Set an appointment for the interview.
- Discuss the procedures to be followed (i.e., who will do what).
- Prepare for the discussion:
  —The employee should prepare his or her own performance assessment.
  —The supervisor should prepare his or her assessment of the employee.
- Assemble job and career planning tools.

The Discussion

- Discuss the employee's performance, and share perceptions of it.
- Negotiate in order to gain concurrence on the performance, if necessary.
- Jointly review the position definition, job standards, and work assignments.
- Establish new or revised objectives.
- Discuss career planning.
- Allow the employee to add his or her comments to the appraisal form.
- Both the evaluator and the employee should sign the forms.

PERFORMANCE EVALUATION AND PLANNING PROCEDURES

Each employee's job performance should be evaluated regularly. This evaluation becomes part of the employee's personnel records and is a factor in compensation, promotion, training, transfer, and termination. The forms shown in Figures 2-4 through 2-14 can be used in preparing for and conducting performance evaluations.

A performance evaluation is a communication tool in that employees are involved in planning their work, targeting performance goals, and measuring results. This allows employees and their immediate supervisors to discuss job performance (as it relates to the desired results) openly. It encourages the discussion of career aspirations and the development of plans toward their realization. It enables the supervisor to evaluate the employee's job performance objectively in terms of the position requirements and other negotiated objectives.

Employee Performance Categories

Explicitly defined terms, such as the following, should be inserted in describing an employee's level of performance:

- *New in Position*—This category includes employees who need more training and/or experience to achieve basic competence levels (e.g., trainees and persons in new positions). An employee should remain in this category until performance and productivity increase through experience. A limit of three months is suggested.
- *Marginal*—This category includes employees whose performance needs improvement to achieve basic competence levels; that is, the performance does not meet minimum job standards or the negotiated objectives. The expected results have not been achieved. Improvement to a competent performance level within a reasonable time is required for the employee to continue in the position.
- *Competent*—This is the standard level of fully adequate performance; that is, the employee's performance meets the previously negotiated objectives. Employees in this category consistently discharge all job requirements in an able manner, and the expected results are achieved.
- *Commendable*—This category includes employees whose job performance exceeds the previously negotiated objectives. The commendable employee is clearly above average in meeting requirements; better-than-expected results are consistently achieved.
- *Distinguished*—Employees in this category have proved themselves exceptional in surpassing objectives. Such employees are outstanding performers whose achievements are readily apparent. These employees are ready for promotion or added responsibilities at an early time.

PERFORMANCE PLANNING

The Performance Planning Interview. The supervisor should prepare for the interview by reviewing:

- The employee's position definition.
- Organizational objectives—This review aids in determining which employee accomplishments are necessary to achieve organizational objectives.
- Appropriate documents prepared by the employee on the job.

The Performance Planning Worksheet. The worksheet should be completed as follows:

- The supervisor and employee should discuss the job standards, in order of importance, that will be used to evaluate the employee's performance (see Figure 2-4).
- Specific objectives that should be met by the employee should be discussed and listed, also in order of importance (see Figure 2-5).
- Common performance factors (i.e., those not related to specific jobs or departments) that are significant for this employee should be checked off (see Figure 2-6); appropriate comments should be added.

PERFORMANCE PLANNING JOB STANDARDS

FOR (EMPLOYEE) DATE

JOB TITLE SUPERVISOR

Here are the job standards we will use to evaluate your performance at your next performance appraisal in _____(Month, Year).

They are in order of their importance.

STANDARDS

EMPLOYEE INITIAL SUPERVISOR INITIAL

Figure 2-4. Performance Planning Worksheet: Job Standards

PERFORMANCE PLANNING SPECIFIC OBJECTIVES

FOR (EMPLOYEE) DATE

JOB TITLE SUPERVISOR

Here are the specific objectives we will use to measure your performance at your next performance appraisal in _____(Month, Year).

They are in order of their importance.

SPECIFIC OBJECTIVES

EMPLOYEE INITIAL SUPERVISOR INITIAL

Figure 2-5. Performance Planning Worksheet: Specific Objectives

PERFORMANCE PLANNING   COMMON PERFORMANCE FACTORS

| FOR (EMPLOYEE) | DATE |
| JOB TITLE | SUPERVISOR |

We will consider the common performance factors checked here in monitoring and evaluating your job performance. These will be considered in addition to, not a replacement for, job standards and objectives.

(NOTE: Only check the most important factors. Use the comment section to further explain level of performance expected and the relative importance of each to overall performance on the job.)

	COMMENTS
☐ QUALITY — of finished work regardless of amount completed. Accuracy, neatness, thoroughness.	
☐ QUANTITY — amount of satisfactory work completed. Volume of output, speed in completing assignments.	
☐ TIME MANAGEMENT — meeting deadlines. Utilizing time effectively for maximum output and/or highest quality. Punctuality. Attendance.	
☐ ORGANIZATION — logically plans and organizes own and/or others' work for most effective handling or reduction of unnecessary activities.	
☐ COMMUNICATIONS — Effectiveness of written, oral, listening skills.	
☐ KNOWLEDGE OF OWN JOB — know-how and skills necessary to do the job. Adequacy of practical, technical, or professional skills and experience.	
☐ KNOWLEDGE OF RELATED AREAS — awareness of work relationships with other areas.	
☐ LEADERSHIP — ability, skills in orienting, motivating, guiding others. Serving as a good example. Optimum use of staff, other resources to complete task, achieve a goal.	
☐ SELF-DEVELOPMENT — awareness of own strengths, weaknesses, interests. Plans for elimination of deficiencies, attainment of goals. Accepts/seeks new responsibilities.	
☐ SELF-STARTER — working with limited supervision or direction. Following through on own initiative.	
☐ HUMAN RELATIONS — effective work relations with supervisor, peers, others outside working unit, favorable customer relations.	
☐ PLANNING — setting objectives, budgeting, scheduling, forecasting.	
☐ DECISION MAKING — making prompt decisions considering relevant factors and evaluating alternatives.	
☐ COST AWARENESS — awareness of financial impact of decisions, actions. Good business judgment.	
☐ DEVELOPING PEOPLE — Recognizing growth potential, development of opportunities, skill in coaching and counseling. Fair and consistent use of discipline. Respect for the individual.	
☐ PERSONNEL PRACTICES — effective and appropriate use of salary and benefits programs, performance appraisal, internal placement, career planning, training and development opportunities, etc.	
☐ AFFIRMATIVE ACTION — working with others harmoniously without regard to race, religion, national origin, sex, age, or handicap. Seeking ways to achieve organizational EEO objectives and timetables. Actively seeking to enhance career objectives of minorities, women and handicapped people.	
☐ SUPPORT OF SOCIAL POLICY, CONSUMER AFFAIRS PROGRAMS — professional, community, or volunteer activities which promote company objectives. Actively promoting Affirmative Lending and other consumer programs.	
☐ OTHER —	

Figure 2-6. Performance Planning Worksheet: Common Performance Factors

Quarterly Reviews. When quarterly reviews are necessary or desirable, the supervisor should review the Performance Planning Worksheet in order to gauge the employee's progress toward achieving the stated goals. The employee should be notified of the review and its expected content at least 24 hours in advance. The following should occur during the review:

- Objectives and desired results should be discussed. If altered circumstances require changing the objectives, new or modified objectives should be inserted at this time (see Figure 2-7).
- The supervisor and the employee should discuss the progress made and complete the appropriate section on the worksheet (see Figure 2-8).

The Performance Planning Worksheet is normally retained within the department after this review.

PERFORMANCE PLANNING

These are the revisions, additions,or deletions we've made and the date of change.

Figure 2-7. Performance Planning Worksheet: Negotiated Objectives

PERFORMANCE APPRAISAL

The performance planning interview, at which objectives should be negotiated between the employee and the supervisor, should be held within three weeks of the last evaluation (these activities can, of course, be done together). The completed Performance Planning Worksheet should be forwarded within one week to the general manager, personnel, and other appropriate departments for review. The worksheet should then be returned to the supervisor.

The Appraisal Form

One week before the scheduled evaluation, the employee should receive copies of the Performance Planning Worksheet and the position description; both documents should be brought to the discussion. The supervisor should complete the appropriate sections on the Performance Appraisal form prior to the interview. The evaluator should compare the results expected (as indicated on the Performance Planning Worksheet) to the achieved results (see Figures 2-9 and 2-10).

PERFORMANCE PLANNING   INTERIM PERFORMANCE REVIEWS

FOR (EMPLOYEE)   JOB TITLE

FIRST REVIEW   DATE _____

EMPLOYEE INITIAL   SUPERVISOR INITIAL

SECOND REVIEW   DATE _____

EMPLOYEE INITIAL   SUPERVISOR INITIAL

THIRD REVIEW   DATE _____

EMPLOYEE INITIAL   SUPERVISOR INITIAL

Figure 2-8. Performance Planning Worksheet: Interim Reviews

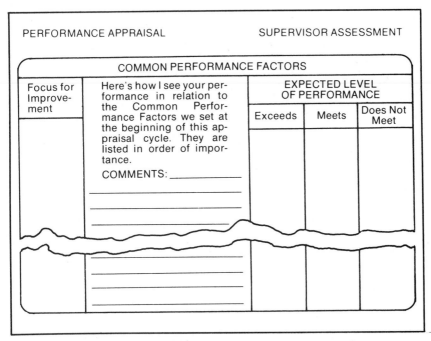

PERFORMANCE APPRAISAL   SUPERVISOR ASSESSMENT

FOR (EMPLOYEE)	JOB TITLE
LOCATION	SUPERVISOR
TIME IN JOB	PERFORMANCE PERIOD: FROM ——— TO ———

SUPERVISOR ASSESSMENT

Here is how I see your performance in relation to the Standards and Objectives we agreed to. They are listed in order of importance.

COMMENTS: _____

EXPECTED LEVEL OF PERFORMANCE

| Exceeds | Meets | Does Not Meet |

Figure 2-9. Performance Appraisal—Supervisor Assessment: Standards and Objectives

PERFORMANCE APPRAISAL   SUPERVISOR ASSESSMENT

COMMON PERFORMANCE FACTORS

| Focus for Improvement | Here's how I see your performance in relation to the Common Performance Factors we set at the beginning of this appraisal cycle. They are listed in order of importance. COMMENTS: _____ | EXPECTED LEVEL OF PERFORMANCE |

| Exceeds | Meets | Does Not Meet |

Figure 2-10. Performance Appraisal—Supervisor Assessment: Common Performance Factors

PERFORMANCE APPRAISAL   SUPERVISOR ASSESSMENT

Here are what I see as your major strengths and abilities, the things you've done particularly well, and the significant improvements you've made since your last appraisal:

_____
_____
_____
_____
_____

I think improvement in these areas will increase your overall effectiveness on the job: (Explain)

_____
_____
_____
_____
_____

I also considered these additional factors (if any) in reaching the overall rating for you:

_____
_____
_____
_____
_____
_____

OVERALL PERFORMANCE

Here's how I rate your overall performance, based on the performance criteria we established and considering the relative importance of each:

DOES NOT MEET   MEETS EXPECTED   EXCEEDS
EXPECTED LEVEL   LEVEL OF   EXPECTED LEVEL
OF PERFORMANCE ☐   PERFORMANCE ☐   OF PERFORMANCE ☐

Figure 2-11. Performance Appraisal—Supervisor Assessment and Rating

Other factors that the evaluator might consider are absences, outside job-related activities, time management, human relations, and such administrative skills as planning, leadership, organizing, and controlling (see Figure 2-11). The overall performance rating (as shown in Figure 2-11) should be the criterion later used to recommend merit increases. The rating should be based on a comparison of the achieved results with the expected results. The supervisor should emphasize the employee's strengths and abilities in relation to his or her job performance (see Figure 2-11). The supervisor should comment on areas in which the employee can upgrade his or her current performance rating and/or be considered for additional responsibilities.

During the discussion the following should occur:

- The evaluator should consider the employee's own assessment (see Figures 2-12 and 2-13) in terms of improving his or her effectiveness in the current position as well as possibly developing the employee for advancement (see Figure 2-14).
- The employee should write any additional comments concerning the evaluation (see Figure 2-14).
- If there is not sufficient time to prepare a Performance Planning Worksheet for the next period (see Figures 2-4 through 2-7), the evaluator and employee should schedule a time within the next three weeks in which to do so.

PERFORMANCE APPRAISAL EMPLOYEE ASSESSMENT

FOR (EMPLOYEE)	JOB TITLE
LOCATION	SUPERVISOR
TIME IN JOB	PERFORMANCE PERIOD: FROM ____ TO ____

EMPLOYEE ASSESSMENT
Here is how I see my performance in relation to Job Standards and Specific Objectives since my last appraisal. They are listed in order of importance.

Figure 2-12. Performance Appraisal—Employee Assessment: Standards and Objectives

PERFORMANCE APPRAISAL   EMPLOYEE ASSESSMENT

I have shown greatest strength or improvement in performing my job in these areas:

_____
_____
_____
_____
_____

I would like to improve my performance on the job in these areas:

_____
_____
_____
_____
_____

These are my objectives for this job, or for a career, or for my own improvement, for now and in the future.
OR: ☐ At this time, I am satisfied in my current position and wish to remain.
(NOTE: This section is optional. By noting your interests, even if they change later on, your supervisor can provide counseling and direction to help you reach your goals.)

_____
_____
_____
_____

Here are ways that would help me improve my performance or meet my objectives (e.g., more or different help from your supervisor, special training in basic or new skills, cross-training in other areas,).

_____
_____
_____
_____
_____

Figure 2-13. Performance Appraisal—Employee Assessment: Strengths and Objectives

PERFORMANCE APPRAISAL   DEVELOPMENT/COMMENTS

DEVELOPMENTAL PLAN

I think we should take these steps to improve your performance on the job or to help you progress toward your personal career objectives.
(Use career planning tools if appropriate. If the employee wants to remain in the present assignment at this time, please say so here.)

EMPLOYEE COMMENTS

What do you think about this appraisal?

EMPLOYEE SIGNATURE   DATE

(Signature indicates you have seen and discussed this appraisal with your supervisor. It does not necessarily imply agreement with the appraisal or overall rating.)

SUPERVISOR'S SIGNATURE   DATE

REVIEWED BY   DATE

ADDITIONAL REVIEW — (If any)   DATE

Figure 2-14. Developmental Plan and Employee Comments

Processing the Performance Appraisal Form

The Performance Appraisal form should be routed to Personnel and other appropriate departments within two days after the interview. The Performance Planning Worksheet covering the period evaluated should be attached.

CONCLUSION

Regular performance appraisals, using the methods and standardized procedures and forms recommended in this chapter, can significantly help employees understand how well they are performing their jobs and how they are perceived by their supervisors. The lack of this information is frequently an important factor in employee dissatisfaction and subsequent resignation.

Such evaluations require time and effort to prepare and execute; the benefits to employees, managers, and the organization, however, can be substantial.

③ Estimating the Cost of Software
by Paul Oliver

THE NECESSITY FOR RESOURCE ESTIMATES

A software estimate is the most knowledgeable statement that can be made about the resources required to develop a software product. It is used in planning to help management decide when to add, delete, or modify resources or when to modify the end product.

A management estimate should be more than a statement of estimated costs. A useful estimate includes time schedules, precise definitions of end products, a list of all pertinent assumptions, and a risk analysis.

The end product of a software development effort is a set of programs and their documentation. Accurate cost and time estimates should be based in part on the estimated program size and characteristics as well as the volume and type of documentation. The assumptions made when estimating constitute an important part of the software plan. Minimally, assumptions must be made about the type and quantity of computer time available.

Three types of estimates must be made during the development cycle. A *feasibility estimate* is a gross estimate used to evaluate trade-offs on alternative approaches. A *commitment estimate* is used to commit resources and make cost/quality trade-offs. An *operational estimate* specifies how project management will use its resources. An operational estimate is an iterative estimate in that it may be modified during a project. Good judgment on which items to incorporate allows use of the same data base and procedures for each of these estimates.

Any sound estimating technique relies, to some extent, on the estimator's experience. The very essence of an estimate is the inference of a relationship between unknown future costs and past experience. There are several basic methods of deriving such a relationship: specific analogy, unit cost, percent of other items, and parametric equations. Note that statistical analysis may or may not be part of these methods.

In using a specific analogy, costs for new software development are estimated by using known costs for previously produced software. The successful application of this method depends on the skills and experience of the estimator, who must be thoroughly familiar with the organization, standards of operation, personnel, programming languages, hardware, and system requirements of the projects used in the analogy. The unit cost method extrapolates the cost per unit of a given resource from a previously determined cost per unit (e.g., the cost of computer time). The percent of other items method sets the cost of a part of a proposed project as a predetermined fraction of the cost of another part. Both the unit cost and the percent of other items methods suffer from the same disadvantages—error magnification and imprecision. Finally, a parametric equation can be used to determine the cost of a proposed project or task. The estimates of time, cost, and effort are functions of required resources and characteristics expected to be present in a project.

Most estimating guidelines rely on the unit cost method of estimating. While this technique is acceptable for operational estimates, previous experience is usually the best guideline when making feasibility estimates. Quantitative formulas are generally not substantiated with respect to the parameters used, and statistics are often presented out of context. One drawback of statistics-based estimates is that they are often based on poor methodology. For example, the fact that an average development project devotes 36 percent of the effort to design does not imply that this is a good allocation of resources. Thus, statistics should not be used blindly; they are not a substitute for good judgment. Finally, on small projects, a manager should be aware that an estimate may actually become a constraint.

THE CURRENT STATUS OF ESTIMATING METHODOLOGY

The most common technique in making operational estimates is the use of experience gained on one or more similar projects. The application of such experience can be remarkably accurate as long as the prior experience was on a project comparable in terms of size, mode, complexity, and application.

Quantitative techniques, of which there are many variations, are commonly used. They all rely on an initial estimate of the size of the project in terms of delivered instructions. Following this, an estimate of programmer productivity is obtained, ideally from an existing data base of past projects. The estimate is then adjusted according to the complexity of the project and other pertinent factors. This done, a man-month requirement is obtained based on the productivity figures and the staffing level for the project. Finally, an additional estimate must be made of the percentage of the total project effort represented by the implementation phase.

Wolverton [1] cites the following breakdowns:

Project	Analysis & Design %	Phase Code & Debug %	Test %
SAGE	39	14	47
NTDS	30	20	50
GEMINI	36	17	47
SATURN V	32	24	44

A rule of thumb is 40-20-40 (i.e., 40 percent of project effort is devoted to analysis and design, 20 percent to coding, and 40 percent to testing). The coding time estimate is generally extrapolated to the entire project. This process has potential pitfalls:

- It relies on an initial estimate of project size that may be inaccurate.
- Accurate productivity figures are often not available.
- The 40-20-40 rule of thumb is not always reliable.
- Adjustments for complexity may simply compound the estimating error.

These considerations notwithstanding, a carefully developed quantitative estimate can be quite accurate if a data base is available consisting of pertinent information gathered from past projects comparable, at least in size, to the one being planned.

A variation on the use of prior experience is to use group estimates that represent an average of individual estimates based on prior experience. Such group estimates can be used for feasibility or resource commitment estimates. The average can give equal weight to the estimate of all participants, or weights can be varied if there are reasons for doing so. Each of the estimators could be asked, for example, to provide a pessimistic, optimistic, and most likely estimate. Giving the most weight to the most likely estimate, a weighted average could be computed. The difficulty with this technique, as with all quantitative techniques, is that it is very easy to lapse into a numbers game, where the production of figures gives the appearance of accuracy even though the figures have little basis in substantive and applicable experience.

Putnam [2] has developed an estimating methodology at the macro level and has had some success in applying this methodology to several Department of the Army projects. His methodology produces the estimates of manpower, cost, and time required to meet critical milestones of software projects. There are four parameters in the basic system. These are in terms managers are comfortable working with—effort, development time, elapsed time, and the state of technology. The system attempts to provide managers with sufficient information to assess the financial risk and investment value of a new software development project before it is undertaken and provides techniques to update estimates once the project is underway.

Putnam's model of the software development life cycle is interesting from an analytic standpoint, but there is little evidence to indicate that it is more accurate as an estimating tool than other works cited in this paper.

Much attention has recently been given to Maurice Halstead's theory, known as software science [3]. The theory attempts to provide precise, objective measures of software complexity; to predict program length; and to estimate the amount of time required to implement a program. This is done by simply counting operators and operands in programs. Despite its apparent simplicity, Halstead's theory has many supporters, and a number of statistical studies have been performed with high correlations between the theory's predictions and actual program measures.

Despite the attention being given to the software estimating problem, it is probably fair to say that no one methodology is close to being as accurate as a businessman or manager would like.

FACTORS THAT INFLUENCE PROGRAMMING

Barry Boehm has provided an excellent picture of the cost factors that affect software and of the cost components of software development [4]. Boehm cites the cost of software to the U.S. Air Force for 1972 alone to be between $1 and $1.5 billion. This is a staggering figure, representing some 70 percent of the Air Force DP budget and nearly five percent of the total Air Force budget. Even considering that the U.S. Air Force is probably not a representative organization, it is safe to suspect that software is an expensive product for any organization.

Even more important is how the cost of software is spread. Boehm's survey indicates that some 40 percent of this cost is in maintenance; it is important, therefore, that we consider the life cycle of software. Boehm also suggests that the following cost factors influence programming:
- Personnel—for whom studies have revealed a productivity ratio between individuals of as much as 26 to 1 [5].
- Management—A manager who knows how to make trade-offs, who can evaluate the implications of using new development tools, and who can make difficult decisions (and recognize when a difficult decision needs to be made) will have a much different impact on the programming for which he is responsible than one who does not possess these qualities.
- Hardware—Strict limitations on hardware resources or execution-speed requirements can seriously affect the programming task, driving software costs upward at an exponential rate.

The programming craft also has an enormous effect on software costs and influences the programming task. Equally important are several new trends that promise to have a strong impact on programming.

Programming Tools and Experience

The use of such programming tools as a programming support library and utility programs has a positive impact on programmer productivity and program reliability. This in turn results in lower system life cycle costs. It is important to stress that costs must be determined over the entire system life cycle, not just over the development phase; programming and support tools require an investment that may or may not be recovered in productivity increases alone, and the positive effects of increased reliability are not realized until the maintenance phase is reached. It is also important that such nonautomated tools as worksheets, standards, and planning and design aids be available.

Programming Language. The programming language and the programmer's experience with the language are also important factors. The technical manager is, unfortunately, faced with several conflicting considerations. For example, COBOL is generally considered superior to FORTRAN for business applications, but compilation times may be more than double for COBOL programs. The manager must weigh suitability of language against resource utilization. It has also been observed that there is no appreciable difference in the amount of training needed to acquire professional competence in the use of a procedural language or an assembly language and that productivity, measured in lines of code produced in a given time period, is roughly the same using either language. This sometimes causes programmers to opt for an assembly language for the sake of the presumably improved object code efficiency. Yet, with a good compiler, a programmer will generally turn out code that is as efficient as the code he would produce using an assembler. Because a procedural language statement explodes into four to eight assembly language statements, there is a substantial increase in productivity. Furthermore, the use of a procedural language improves the communication of algorithms between programmers and facilitates the transfer of programs between computer types.

Regardless of the programming language used, the experience of a programmer with the language is an important factor in both productivity and reliability. Also important are the experiences of the programming team with a similar application and with the target computer.

Nelson [6] gives us a measure of just how important some of these factors can be. He cites a difference of as much as 40 percent in program run time attributable to programmer experience and an even greater discrepancy in memory utilization. Nelson also cites up to 90 percent reduction in coding costs resulting from the use of decision tables. This saving is obtained by obviating the use of flowcharts and by improved system design and checkout procedures.

Interactive Programming. A particularly important trend affecting cost estimating is online interactive programming. Edward Lias reported on an experiment conducted to measure the impact of online programming on life cycle costs [7]. Sackman has also collected data on a number of independent studies of this issue [5]. Generally, comparative results were quite close, indicating that using the same programming techniques online does not significantly improve programmer productivity. Detractors of online systems have also pointed out that, besides the higher costs of interactive programming, there is the danger of overusing the computer to compensate for poor design and planning by careless development and program testing.

Environmental Factors

The environment in which programming takes place has an impact on the cost of programming and the programming task itself. Computer turnaround time for jobs submitted by project personnel affects productivity, reliability of programs, and work habits. It is better for the programmer to have one big block of time with concentrated access to the system than several cracks at the computer during the day. Unfortunately, block time is seldom available in this era of online systems and time sharing. One successful mode of operation is 24-hour turnaround time: the programmer knows that he will not get his output for a given run until the next day and devotes his time to other work, without further concern for the job related to the run submitted.

A disciplined environment is, in the short run, a more costly one (developing and enforcing standards and procedures is costly) but leads, in the long run, to more efficient and reliable software that is produced more rapidly. This is also true with regard to disciplined use of supplies, work space, storage space, and the like.

Continuity is important to a software development project. There are two cost factors that can disrupt continuity: personnel turnover and travel. Personnel turnover creates obvious problems. The disrupting influence of frequent travel on the part of the programming staff is sometimes not recognized. There is a loss of productivity during travel as well as some time before and after each trip.

Application Factors

The nature of the system being developed affects timeliness, reliability, and resource requirements for a software development project. Some of the more significant factors in this category are:

- Data file characteristics—for example, the number and types of fields in each input and output format for the system being developed, the number of nonoverlapping fields used to define the data base for a system (i.e., the number of distinct formats), the number of input and output formats.
- Size of the project—the number of lines of source code and the number of programs in the system.
- Complexity of the project—whether the end product is system software or an application system, the number of branches in a program, the number of source code updates.
- Volume of documentation—This includes the system definition; functional specifications and descriptions; user guides; test specifications; and design, implementation, and evaluation documentation.

THE PROBLEMS WITH CURRENT ESTIMATING TECHNIQUES

Limitations of Historical Data. The consensus among experts is that the major source of difficulty in making accurate estimates is the lack of adequate historical data. This is due, in large part, to the fact that programming is an infant discipline. In addition, the existing data is not fully comprehended. The economics of programming are not well understood, nor is the nature of large systems. Thus, a major task for the software development manager is to better comprehend the cost factors that influence the programming activity in his organization and, concomitantly, to create an organizational and procedural structure that delineates these factors.

Although we have some data on the software development process, it is fragmentary and inconclusive. Kosy, for example, compiled the available data on productivity for the Air Force Command and Control Information Processing study [8]. His summary covers the period from 1960 to 1970 and includes the Bell Labs Electronic Switching System No. 1, the IBM OS/360 project, and the Multics project. It is difficult, however, to arrive at any meaningful conclusions from the figures given. Consider, for example, the following:

- Productivity on 169 System Development Corporation programs ranged from 100 to 1,000 machine instructions per man-month. What caused the variability? What factors influenced the productivity? The questions are not answered by the data.

- The Multics-2 project reveals a productivity of some 100 instructions per man-month, but these are in a higher-level language, and the productivity ratio includes the system design and integration testing phases. How does this figure relate to the SDC data?

- The OS/360 project data shows a productivity of less than 100 machine instructions per man-month, but the size of OS/360 was 10 times that of Multics-2, and its development effort (in man-months) was nearly 50 times that of Multics-2.

What is one to conclude from this data? To say simply that large systems (e.g., OS/360) are more difficult to develop than smaller ones (e.g., Multics-2) is hardly a startling revelation. Furthermore, we do not know the details of what was being measured in these projects. For some, the figures cited account for the entire development process (including design and testing); for others, the figures apply only to the implementation phase of the software project.

One of the most thorough data collection efforts was performed by SDC in the mid-1960s. In his handbook of cost estimates [6], Nelson points out the limitations of even this large data base. The data is representative of only the design, code, and test phases of software development. Extrapolated estimates of time and cost for analysis, preparation, acceptance testing, documentation, and the like would not necessarily be accurate. A second problem with the SDC study is that the data is subject to a large standard error. The programs sampled varied in size from 150 instructions to 217,000, the effort levels ranged from 1 to 300 man-months, and productivity ranged from 10 to 13,889 machine instructions per man-month. It is obvious that such factors as program size, complexity, and programmer skills had an impact on the statistics, but the extent of that impact is not clear from the data. Perhaps most important, the data in this and similar studies does not reflect changing technology.

Limitations on the Understanding of the Product. Although certain measures of software have been quantified (e.g., cost, speed in performing a given function on a given system, size, effort to produce, time to produce, and resource utilization), most have not. As every manager knows, unfortunately, there are many critical characteristics that have not been quantified because there is no way to measure them. We have, for example, no generally applicable definition of software reliability, nor is acceptability (generality or flexibility) of a software package amenable to precise measurement. The time and effort required to modify a system, either to use it in a different environment or to maintain it in its native environment, cannot be accurately estimated, nor can system integrity (i.e., the degree to which the operation of one program can protect the operation of another).

Equally critical is the lack of fundamental principles governing the scope and complexity of software functions. There have been attempts to analyze the computational efficiency of software, but these techniques are too limited to apply to practical software systems. As Brooks points out [9], the very tractability of the medium has created a situation in which there may be no theoretical limits on software production techniques.

Limitations on the Management of People. Hardware production is a well-defined process, and the individual on the production line has precisely defined tasks to perform with no provisions for creativity. It is the nature of programmers, on the other hand, to do interesting work (e.g., design and coding) at the expense of dull work (e.g., testing and documenting). Past practices in the profession have led to a persistent attitude that doing the job in a clever way is often considered more important than doing it on time, adequately, and within the constraints of cost and resource utilization.

Programmers and software development managers also tend to be optimistic. They often consider the bulk of a project to be the production of code (in fact, it comprises about 20 percent of the task) and regard planning, design, and testing as minor adjuncts.

LaBolle makes an interesting comparison between buying or producing television sets and buying or producing software [10]. The buyer of a television set can enter a store and choose from many models. The buyer can observe and compare the models, consult with others regarding the relative quality of these models, read descriptive literature and comparisons prepared by commercial publications, and readily obtain data on reliability, weight, power consumption, and ease of use. There are, however, no broadly applicable standards for comparing computer programs. Computer programs are developed from functional specifications that lack quantitative measures, and there seldom exists reliable descriptive information on them.

A manager responsible for producing television sets benefits from standard parts and terminology, proven techniques for predicting and measuring performance, a voluminous data base that can be used to predict what to expect from the workers on the assembly line, and proven quality control techniques. The manager of software development is faced with an absence of standards for products, components of products, activities, manpower requirements, and performance measures.

RECOMMENDED POLICIES AND PROCEDURES

Accurate estimates cannot be made except within the context of sound project management. Sound project management requires a formal structure within the software project and uniform management procedures and development methodologies. A data base of information on past projects is of limited use, unless such uniform conditions exist. The development cycle must first be divided into a standard set of phases so that meaningful comparisons between projects are possible. The following list is representative:

- Definition—The technical problem is defined, and a plan is produced. A baseline design may be initiated, but the emphasis at this time is on what is to be solved rather than on how to solve it.
- Design—A proposed solution is adopted after evaluation of the alternatives. The project plan and baseline design are completed. The detailed design and preparation for all testing are initiated.
- Production—Programs are developed and tested. Unit and integration testing are completed, as is all program documentation. Preparation for system testing (i.e., validation performed by a separate quality assurance group) is completed. Preparation for acceptance testing continues.
- System testing—Integration testing is repeated, using different data in a live environment, by a separate quality assurance group. Any required customer training is initiated.
- Acceptance testing—Systems and related documentation are presented to the customer for formal acceptance according to predefined criteria.
- Installation and operation—Systems are installed in their operational environment, retested as required, and put into operation.
- Maintenance—Enhancements, modifications, and corrections are made over the remaining life of the system.

From these life cycle phases, we can define functional requirements that a project management system must satisfy. The system should include policies, procedures, standards, guidelines, methodologies, and tools that enable project managers to:

- Identify resources, schedules, and deliverables; make accurate estimates of costs associated with manpower, computer time, publications, travel, relocation, equipment, and checkpoints; develop budget control procedures, project budgets by resource and accounts, and operating budgets.
- Define a meaningful reporting structure that includes internal and external reviews and provides reports from nonmanagers, technical managers, and task or project managers.
- Divide the task accomplishment cycle into meaningful phases, defining primary and secondary objectives for each.
- Define a project organization from a series of alternatives, evaluating the advantages and disadvantages of each.
- Define testing levels and establish objectives, procedures, responsibilities, and tools for each.
- Define procedures to be used in controlling changes, defining baseline documents, establishing change control boards, and implementing customer-initiated changes.
- Define procedures and resources required for all project publications and outline the basic set of project documents.
- Develop external and internal training programs in support of the project.
- Develop procedures for the installation and operation of completed systems.

- Acquire and evaluate technical data for projecting schedules and re-source requirements, including planning versus actual data; data to define, design, implement, and evaluate systems; data on the system environment; and data at the system, subsystem, and module levels.

Such a project management system is essential if management estimates are to have any degree of accuracy.

Estimating Guidelines

The guidelines listed below can be used for estimating large software development projects. This includes any project that involves more than eight full-time professionals and whose eventual size will exceed 100,000 lines of source code.

System Design Phase [11]
- Requirements analysis—5 to 19 man-weeks, depending on the nature of the project
- Total system design—one to three man-months
- Software system design—10 percent of total man-months
- Review of system design with user—three man-days per design document
- Training—one month for programmers if analysts turn over design to programmers

Production [11]
- Develop system test plan—one man-month per 10,000 estimated instructions
- Program design—one man-month per 1,000 instructions
- Program file design—one man-month per 10,000 items
- Establish system files (used by more than one program)—two man-months per 10,000 machine instructions
- Program coding—gross estimates: one man-month per 5,000 machine instructions

Program Testing [11]
- Familiarization with procedures—one week
- Individual program testing—approximately 20 percent of the testing effort
- Subsystems testing—from 0 to 30 percent of the total testing effort, depending on the number of subsystems
- System testing—approximately 50 percent of testing effort; about 25 percent of total effort

Design, Coding, Debugging, and Testing Estimating
The following formulas can be used to determine the man-months required for program design through testing:

$$\text{man-months} = 5.2 \left(x \quad \begin{array}{c} \text{The Number of Thousands of} \\ \text{Source Code Instructions} \end{array} \right)^{0.91} \quad [12]$$

<u>or</u>

$$\text{man-months} = 4.495 \times \left(\begin{array}{c}\text{The Number of Thousands of} \\ \text{Source Code Instructions}\end{array}\right)^{0.781} \quad [13]$$

Note that the second formula is to be used for small business systems where the number of source code instructions is to be less than 10,000.

Project Administration and Data Collection. Guidelines for data collection and reporting represent a most essential support component. Accurate, timely, and uniformly understood data is needed by managers at all levels for the planning, organization, and control of a project and for the communication of project information within and outside the project structure. Guidelines are applicable to all levels of management in a software development project since the information requirements of all managers are essentially the same, differing only in the level of detail required.

Managers are cautioned that there are several problems regarding project data that require flexibility on their part. The most difficult of these problems is a lack of understanding of what the software development and management process should be. The many studies on the subject emphasize the difficulty and complexity of the process but have done little to reveal a well-defined methodology or to delineate precise relationships among project variables. Thus, we do not know precisely what data is required, when it is required, or in what form it is required to enable managers to make sound estimates. Such knowledge, however, will come not from additional studies but from the monitoring, evaluation, and refinement or modification of established procedures.

A related problem is that of defining programmer productivity, since most estimates discussed here relate to the determination and prediction of productivity. Quantity of source code produced, expressed in terms of lines of code per time period, has been the most widely accepted measure but has never become an industry standard. One problem with this definition is its lack of precision. This is not a particularly serious problem, however, since greater precision would simply be a matter of interpretation. A more serious problem is the narrowness of the definition. There is ample evidence to suggest that a good definition of productivity should have elements that address the correctness, efficiency, and complexity of programs.

Finally, data collection and reporting requirements are implemented together with certain development methodologies that can be lumped under the term structured programming technology. Such technology requires increased collecting, analysis, and reporting of management data and, to be truly effective, requires the support of a software development library. A library allows data items to be collected and counted in a standardized manner and a focal point (the librarian) to be established for manually collected data items and as a source of control on the collection process. Note that a library facilitates the merging of technical and management or administrative data. Such a development library, however, requires a disciplined approach to development, which is not always welcomed.

A reporting system uses as input a base of estimated and actual data on a project's environment, system module descriptions, resource costs, processing resources, and program production. The data is gathered and stored in a computerized data base. Data is added to, deleted from, or replaced from this data base during the course of a project. Additional capabilities must exist for summarizing, sorting, and otherwise processing the data. Reports are generated and disseminated for project support and historical purposes. Thus, the functional requirements of the system can be expressed as processing functions: collecting, updating, processing, reporting, and archiving.

Two classes of data are required to plan and manage a project: planned data is developed during the planning phase of a project and is derived in part from actual data on previous projects; actual data is collected during the course of the project. Within these two classes, five types of data should be collected:

- Project environment—general data of a static nature, defining the scope of the project.
- Module descriptions—data that is usually automatically collected and that applies to programs, subprograms, and units of a system.
- Service data—This type of data is limited to turnaround time for various sources of computer service.
- Cost data—All cost data, from personnel costs to travel costs, falls into this category.
- Production data—includes all characteristics related to the production of source code and includes quality assurance and programming data (e.g., categories of source-code updates, enhancements, changes to functional requirements, and errors).

A project manager requires information on the general project characteristics, project and program status, quality of the products produced, use of resources, and adherence to standards and guidelines. The following report classes provide this information:

- Statistics on programs, subprograms, and units
- Production statistics
- Use of computer resources
- System design/program structure
- Historical/summary data
- Combinations of the preceding

Certain reports should be produced on a fixed reporting cycle. This is determined by management and usually depends on customer requirements. All reports should be available upon request. Project managers should be responsible for all data collection and reporting activities but should delegate some authority for collection and reporting to the appropriate organizational levels or functions within the project.

Management Reporting. The contents of management reports are derived from the data items previously listed and from calculations based on these items. The reports defined here are primarily technical in nature and deal with the project per se:

- Status Reports—used by managers in determining the status of the

source code during production and testing phases
- Update Reports—used by programmers and managers in tracking unit, program, and system update activity during production and testing
- Time Reports—used by managers in monitoring, optimizing, and allocating computer test time during the design and production phases
- Project History—used by prospective project managers and middle management for planning and control purposes
- System Cost Reports—used by managers at all levels, but principally by project managers, in the monitoring of development costs

FUTURE DIRECTIONS

It is clear that the software manager faces a lack of adequate historical data on completed software development projects, a lack of precise understanding of the variables influencing programming, and an inability to determine just how much work is to be accomplished on a given software development project. Furthermore, few standards and management controls are enforced.

There have been a few significant trends in programming during the past 15 to 20 years. The use of online systems is one of these, and it has already been discussed. Structured programming is another, more fundamental trend. Whatever the merits of the various components of structured programming, the many experiments with this discipline represent the first serious attempt at understanding programming and its many aspects; more important, they imply the recognition that programming is not simply a tool to be used by subject matter specialists but is a discipline in its own right.

Structured programming technology includes [14]:
- Top-down structured programming
- Program support libraries
- Program design languages (PDLs)

Although it does not currently appear that the use of PDLs has a significant bearing on estimating techniques, given the importance of system design, their use should be significant. It is too early, however, to evaluate the extent of this impact.

The use of top-down structured programming will, on the other hand, definitely help the standards and control problem because it *is* a set of standards and controls. Top-down development and integration reduces or eliminates the unpredictable cost elements of redoing interfaces and modules, hence alleviating the problem of work determination. Unfortunately, we do not yet have enough experience to know the magnitude of these effects. It is equally unfortunate that structured programming does not appear to have any direct impact on our understanding of the factors affecting programming, although the data collection inherent in using a programming support library may eventually bear some fruit. Note that the development and use of a programming support library can be invaluable in collecting data on software projects, with such data to be used on future projects for estimating purposes.

The Critical Nature of Requirements

Many groups involved in the development of new programming languages have concentrated on giving the programmer a greater variety of tools with which to express programs. Recently, however, evidence shows that the most serious software errors are caused by problems in requirements engineering and design specification and that coding errors are best avoided by simplifying programs and languages, not by adding to them. The severity of these problems can be appreciated by noting that, according to data gathered at TRW [15], requirements specifications errors not found until a system is in operation can be as much as 50 times more costly to repair than those recognized during the requirements specifications phase itself. In addition to the repair cost problems, the lack of good requirements specifications causes other difficulties:

- Top-down design is extremely difficult when there is no well-defined "top."
- Testing is difficult if one is testing against ill-defined specifications.
- It is difficult to convince users and management that they are really a part of the development effort if what is being developed is poorly specified.

Present Status and Future Technology

Software requirements are generally written in free-form English, an ambiguous form of communication. Such terms as real time, sufficient, and reliable abound, as do more precise-sounding but equally vague terms as 99 percent reliable. Determination of requirements, when done well, is usually performed using various ad hoc techniques and common sense. When such determination is done poorly, it generally follows guidelines dictated by preconceptions.

Recent years have seen attempts at ameliorating this situation with the development of specification languages and automatic programming systems. Teichroew and Sayani [16] reported what is probably the pioneer system for specifying software requirements in a machine analyzable way. While this system (ISDOS) was developed primarily for business systems applications, its concepts apply to any application area. This system uses a Problem Statement Language, which allows a designer to specify a system using a set of formalized primitives (e.g., inputs, outputs, and updates) and a Problem Statement Analyzer, which can produce statistics, directories of key words, and other useful summaries.

There has also been a growing interest in automatic programming, motivated partly by the desire to bring some sanity to software production and partly by the realization, due largely to the work of Dijkstra [17], Mills [18], and others, that sanity is possible.

CONCLUSION

The impact of many factors and trends on programming costs is acknowledged but poorly understood. Some of the most important questions requiring further study and understanding are:

- What is the productivity of the average programmer, and what factors affect it? How do we know when we have identified the proper parameters? Given data on a specific project, how do we know if a resulting productivity is caused by project complexity or poor design? Is a high error rate a result of project size or poor functional specifications?
- What impact does complexity have on a software project? Wolverton [1] cites an increase in the cost of a complex project (e.g., a real-time project) ranging from 3 to 5.5 times the average, but we do not know what factors contribute how much to complexity.
- What resource constraints (e.g., memory or execution-time limitations) affect productivity and reliability?
- How does productivity vary with programmer ability, and what effect will the Chief Programmer Team concept have on this?

The manager of software development can do much to answer some of these questions for his organization. Adopting a structured programming methodology is a good place to start, particularly using a programming support library. Of the other factors likely to be influential, the following should receive the closest attention:

- The use of programming support tools
- Precise specification of functional requirements
- Programming languages
- Test turnaround time
- Programming practices and standards
- Number of lines of source code
- Project complexity
- Volume of documentation
- Number of files per program
- Access methods and data structures for files

Once gathered, this information should be augmented by similar data obtained, as available, from sources outside the organization. The manager can then adapt the programming practices in his organization to improve productivity and reliability of the software developed under his management.

References

1. Wolverton, R.W. "The Cost of Developing Large Scale Software." TRW-SS-72-01 (March 1972).
2. Putnam, L.H. "A General Empirical Solution to the Macro Software and Estimating Problem." *IEEE Transaction on Software Engineering.* Vol SE-4, No. 4 (July 1978).
3. Halstead, G.H. *Elements of Software Science.* New York: Elsevier North-Holland Inc, 1977.
4. Boehm, B.W. "The High Cost of Software." *Proceedings of a Symposium on the High Cost of Software.* Stanford Research Institute, Menlo Park CA, 1973.
5. Sackman, H. *Man-Computer Problem Solving.* Pennsauken, NJ: Auerbach Publishers, 1970.
6. Nelson, E.A. "Management Handbook for the Estimation of Computer Programming Cash." SDC, Santa Monica CA, 1967.
7. Lias, E.J. "On-Line vs. Batch Costs." *Datamation,* (December 1974).
8. Kosy, D.W. "Air Force Command and Control Information Processing in the 1980s: Trends in Software Technology." R-1012-PR, Rand Corporation, 1974.
9. Brooks, F.P. Jr. "Why is the Software Late?" *Data Management* (August 1971), 18-21.
10. LaBolle, V. "Estimation of Computer Programming Costs." SDC, Santa Monica CA, 1964.
11. Farr, L., LaBolle, V., and Norman Withworth. *Planning Guide for Computer Program Development.* SDC, Santa Monica CA, 1965.
12. Walston, C.E., and C.P. Felix. "Programming Measurement and Estimation." *IBM Systems Journal.* No. 1 (1977).
13. Doty Associates, Inc. "Software Cost Estimation Study." Vol. 1, 2 (June 1977).
14. Structured Programming Series. "Programming Language Standards." RADC-TR-74-300, Vol. 1, 1974.
15. Boehm, B.W. "Software Engineering." TRW-SS-76-08, October 1976.
16. Teichroew, D. and Sayani, H. "Automation of System Building." *Datamation,* (August 1971), 25-30.

17.   Dijkstra, Edsger. *A Discipline of Programming*. Englewood Cliffs NJ: Prentice-Hall, 1976.
18.   Mills, Harlan *Structured Programming*. Reading MA: Addison-Wesley, 1979.

Bibliography

Baker, F.T. "Chief Programmer Team Management of Production Programming." *IBM Systems Journal*. Vol. 2, No. 1 (1972), 56-73.

4 Designing Modular Programs

by Kathryn Heninger
and John E. Shore

INTRODUCTION

In system design, a module is a self-contained unit that performs a specific task or set of tasks in support of the overall system operation. If the allocation of tasks to modules is well done and the module interfaces well defined, modules can be built and tested independently. Even after they are integrated into a system, individual modules can be modified or replaced independently. As a result, modifications to improve performance or change functionality can be made much more easily with a modular system than with a nonmodular counterpart.

The advantages of modularity are routinely achieved for computer hardware but not for computer software. The reason for this is that hardware development is governed to a much larger degree by intrinsic constraints that impose discipline on the design process. Such physical characteristics as layout, connections, and power, for example, place limits on design alternatives. These constraints have resulted in accepted standards for component design.

In contrast, the software design medium fails to impose an inherent discipline. Far from following standard practices, software professionals cannot even agree on a definition for software modules. Although many people equate software modules with subroutines, there is growing recognition that subroutines are not necessarily self-contained and cannot necessarily be built and modified independently. This chapter presents a different view—a software module is a collection of programs and data that takes care of one separately changeable aspect of a system. Because input data formats frequently change, for instance, all programs in a system that must know a particular input format in order to read data belong in one module.

Based on this definition of module, this chapter discusses the basics of modular program design. Some common software development problems that can be alleviated by modular program design are presented and basic concepts introduced. Also presented is a step-by-step methodology for modular design and a discussion of the performance issues related to modular program design, as well as related management considerations.

THE EFFECT OF MODULAR DESIGN ON LIFE-CYCLE PROBLEMS

Figure 4-1 shows the major stages in the life cycle of a software product. Because of short-term pressures, the design phase is often shortchanged. As a result, software projects commonly suffer from unpredicted delays and cost overruns in the programming and integration stages and produce programs that are unreliable and hard to modify.

In contrast, modular design methods require that substantial effort be expended in the design stage so that the software structure is developed systematically and documented thoroughly. This effort can alleviate the problems described in the following paragraphs by making the programs easier to code, integrate, and maintain. The advantages do not come automatically, however; modular design principles do not provide a foolproof algorithm for software design. A good design requires that these principles be applied intelligently, since each application area presents its own special design problems.

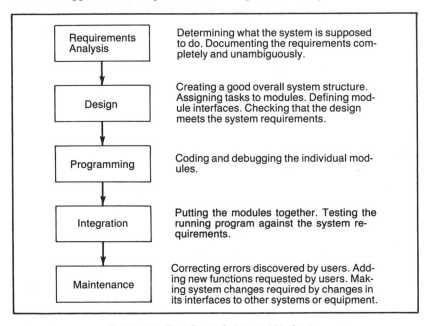

Figure 4-1. Five-Stage Software Life Cycle

Problem 1: Making Changes is Costly. Software can be so difficult to change that it is cheaper to reprogram it entirely. It is often difficult to find the right code sections to change, either because the original structure is hard to understand or because it has become lost beneath layers of patches. Changes to one part of a program often have a ripple effect, causing errors in apparently unrelated parts. When changes are not followed by exhaustive retesting, new versions can be released with errors that were introduced in the maintenance process. Many of these problems can be traced to failure to anticipate change.

Programmers suffer from a common illusion that software requirements will at some point be frozen. Functional requirements and system interfaces are never completely fixed; they change frequently during all stages of the life cycle. There are many reasons for this: the original requirements are often too complicated to be spelled out completely, and specification techniques are often too primitive to ensure that all aspects will be covered adequately. In addition, changes in user needs, new operating system releases, and hardware result in required modifications even to the well-specified aspects of the system.

Modular Programming Can Help. Unanticipated changes can invalidate basic but implicit assumptions made throughout a program, requiring alteration of many parts of the code. Modular programming techniques can be used to isolate code sections associated with a particular change so that they are self-contained, easy to find, and reasonably small. Unless changes must be made in module interfaces, a programmer can be confident that modifications will not cause subtle errors to be introduced into other parts of the system. It is impossible to design a program so that any conceivable change is easy. If it is possible to identify classes of changes that are likely to occur, however, it is possible to design a program so that changes are easy to make.

Problem 2: Staff Communication and Training are Costly. According to Brooks' law[1], "Adding manpower to a late software project makes it later." This phenomenon is caused partly by an increase in the overhead of staff communication and partly by the cost of training new programmers.

The amount of time spent in staff communication depends to some extent on how interrelated the separate programming assignments are. If programs are highly interrelated, programmers must spend time learning of each other's problems and approaches; otherwise, their individual products will not fit together correctly. It is common for a project to depend dangerously on the few key people who understand how the whole system works. Not only are these people constantly distracted from their work by questions from other programmers, but the project is delayed by their absences.

Additional problems are caused by the high turnover rates characteristic of programming departments. Training new people is time-consuming, expensive, and does not contribute directly to progress. If programs are so interrelated that a new programmer must understand most of the system before working on even a small part of it, it may be months before that programmer can make a contribution to the project.

Modular Programming Can Help. Modular programming results in the division of a project into small, well-documented, manageable tasks. This division limits the amount of information that any one person must know and reduces the dependencies among members of a software team. Programmers of different modules can proceed without constantly referring to each other's work. Training is easier since programmers can make progress without understanding the whole system.

Problem 3: Integration is Often Unexpectedly Difficult. The system integration stage can be a nightmare. Because of omissions, misunderstandings, and unstated assumptions made during the design and programming stages, components that pass their individual checkout tests can fail to work when they are put together, and it can be very difficult to determine why. Frequently, every programmer must participate in this process because no one except the authors of particular components understands those components.

Modular Programming Can Help. Modular programming techniques can lead to fewer surprises during system integration because well-modularized software is characterized by simple interfaces and clear allocation of responsibility. By reviewing module specifications before coding starts, many ambiguities and misunderstandings can be discovered before they are built into the individual components. As a result, a module that passes its unit tests is more likely to fit smoothly into the overall system. Because the individual modules are well documented, the problems that do occur are not difficult to trace.

Problem 4: Documentation is Either Useless or Not Produced at All. Because it is typically not performed by the same programmers who develop a system, software maintenance can be made much more difficult by poor documentation. Software documentation is typically written as an afterthought by programmers who are poor writers or by writers who are poor programmers. Even if the programmers write it willingly, documentation for a muddled design cannot be clear. Useless documentation is almost worse than none; it gives management false confidence that the information needed to maintain the software is available.

Modular Programming Can Help. Documentation should be written as software is developed so that it captures the fundamental reasons behind the design. Feedback from the writing can improve the design. If an aspect of the design cannot be described clearly, it can usually be designed better. Relevant information tends to disappear if it is not written down while the design is in progress; notes get lost, and people forget the factors that influence design decisions. Modular programming techniques dictate that documentation be the only product of the design stage; not until the documentation is approved can coding begin. Careful documentation is an integral part of modular programming methods.

Reusing the Results of Modular Programming. An additional advantage of modular programming is the reusability of some of its products. Well-defined modules that perform such common functions as sorting or statistical calculations can often be used without modification in other systems. Moreover, one can sometimes take an overall modular design and reuse it for a similar system by adapting some of the modules to the new circumstances.

BASIC CONCEPTS

In this section, some fundamental concepts of modular programming are introduced. Several of them are illustrated through a simple example—a mailing list program. The requirements of this program are to maintain a file of addresses and to generate mailing lists of addresses selected from the file. Mailing lists produced by the system need not contain all names in the file; the system is to select records that match predefined criteria (e.g., those with the title ''Doctor''). The address file is to be assembled from different sources, including magazine subscription lists and organization membership lists. These lists are all in machine-readable form, but their record formats vary. The system, therefore, must be able to process inputs with different formats and must be easy to modify for the processing of new input formats. In order to give clients a selection, various print formats must be available. It also must be easy to add new print formats.

Modules

A module is a collection of related programs and data structures that take care of a single changeable aspect of a system. The programs within a module are all based on information that is not used in the design of other programs in the system. This information is termed the *secret* of the module (see Figure 4-2). Another good example of this would be a tape-handler module of an operating system, which would contain the programs to read a record, write a record, and rewind the tape. All three programs would be based on information about how a specific tape drive device behaves, including transmission protocols, validity checking, and timing.

Modules that isolate information are sometimes called information-hiding modules [2]. The two main advantages of information-hiding modules are that they simplify the rest of the system because it does not refer to the hidden details and the encapsulated aspect of the system can be changed by replacing only one module. For example, application programs are simpler because they use the tape-handler programs; they can write on a tape without knowing the details of the hardware interface to the device. Substituting a new tape drive model can be done without changing all of the application programs that store data on tape; only the tape-handler module need be rewritten. Note that these modules are not necessarily equivalent to single subroutines, nor do they consist entirely of programs. They may also include data bases, job control language, or compile-time parameters.

Software modules serve two complementary purposes: they are units in the software structure (i.e., units that can be changed independently), and they are units in the programming process (i.e., independent work assignments). A good module for one purpose is generally a good module for the other because both depend on clear definitions of module tasks and interfaces. Both purposes should be considered during module design.

The maintainability of a system depends on how well it is divided into units of software change. If this division is done well, a change will require that only one module be reprogrammed, without requiring any changes in the rest of the system.

The rate of programming progress can be affected significantly by how well the system is divided into work assignments. If this division is done well, each

Module Name	Module Type	Responsibility	Secret	What Might Cause the Secret to Change
Address Storage Module	Facility	Stores and retrieves address data associated with each person in the file.	Hides the choice of data structure used to represent the file in the computer, how the information for a given individual is arranged, and whether or not the file is all in main memory or stored partly on disk.	These choices may change because the time/space trade-offs are affected by changes in the size of the address file, in the availability of memory, or in the required access speed.
Input Device Module	Facility	Reads records or characters from an input device (e.g., tape drive, OCR, card reader).	Hides commands and data formats expected by the device (e.g., EBCDIC vs. ASCII).	Changes if the device is replaced by a new model.
Input Format Module	Facility	Uses programs in the input device module to read in addresses; analyzes input records into component parts and stores them in the address holder.	Hides the format of the input data, including the arrangement of the fields, the field delimiters, end-of-record delimiters, size of fields, etc.	May change because many machine-readable address lists are available, and the lists have different formats.
Output Device Module	Facility	Writes characters or strings to an output device (e.g., printer).	Hides commands and data formats expected by the device (e.g., EBCDIC vs. ASCII).	Changes if the device is replaced by a new model.
Output Format Module	Facility	Uses output device module programs to write addresses in a selected format.	Hides details of the format, including spacing, arrangement, and supplied punctuation.	May change because different clients want their mailing lists printed differently; even the requirements of the same client change over time.
Selection Module	Facility	Determines, for a given address, whether or not it belongs in a particular set (e.g., all Maryland residents).	Hides the specific criteria used to make the decision.	Criteria vary because different clients require mailing lists with different subsets of the people in the file.
Command Format Module	Facility	Uses programs in the input device module to read in a command from a user; interprets commands.	Hides the format and source of user input (e.g., whether options are on JCL cards, on an extra input data file, or from a terminal). Hides the defaults assumed if user fails to supply commands.	May change because user finds one format awkward or because he wants different defaults.
Master Control Module	Control	Calls programs in all other modules to get the job done.	Hides the sequence of actions required to meet the overall system requirements.	

Figure 4-2. Mailing List Program Example—Modules and Their Secrets

unit will be sufficiently self-contained to be performed by a single programmer, with very little interaction with other programmers. In order for a module to be self-contained, its purpose, function, and interfaces to other modules must be precisely defined. Otherwise, programmers will spend much of their time negotiating with each other about who is responsible for what and how information is to be transmitted among programs. If the system is properly partitioned, programmers can make progress independently most of the time, with a minimum of time wasted waiting for or talking to others.

If the software system is very large, it may have several teams of programmers working on it. In this case, it should be divided into large modules that can be assigned to different teams, and each of these modules should be divided into modules for individual programmers.

Different modules often require programmers with different expertise. If the various talents of the available programmers are considered during the module design process, there can be a payoff in terms of efficient use of people. This consideration should be secondary to the considerations involving ease of change, however, partly because the ease of change affects the whole life cycle and partly because the people available tend to change even during the programming stage.

Each module is a building block of the entire software system and must therefore cooperate with other modules in order to meet the requirements placed on the system as a whole. There are two main types of modules. Facility modules provide a facility or resource that makes the rest of the software easier to program. The secrets of these modules can be details about peripheral devices, data structures, or algorithms. Control modules use the facilities in order to meet overall system requirements. The secrets of these modules are the sequences of actions required.

Module Hierarchy

Even if modules have clearly defined tasks and interfaces, the sheer number of them can make the system hard to understand unless they are organized in some way. An appropriate organization is a module hierarchy (see Figure 4-3): the relationship between a module and its parent in the hierarchy is ''part of.'' Modules thus belong to module classes, and the module classes may themselves be viewed as modules. At the top of the hierarchy is a small number of large modules or module classes that together meet the system requirements. Each of these modules is subdivided into smaller, more specialized modules that together meet the requirements of the parent module, and so on. The modules at the lowest level are so simple that subdividing them further does not make the system easier to understand.

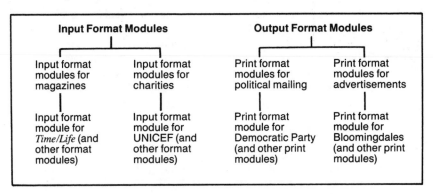

Figure 4-3. Part of the Mailing List Module Hierarchy

A module hierarchy allows a person to learn about a system by first reading about the top-level modules, seeing how they cooperate to meet the top-level requirements, and then studying the child modules of one module, seeing how they cooperate to meet its requirements, and so on. The reader need consider only a small number of modules at a time. A maintenance programmer can find the way to the right module in order to make a change by starting at the top, selecting the appropriate top-level module, and then selecting the appropriate submodule at each intermediate level until the appropriate lowest-level module is reached. At any level, the programmer has only a small number of modules from which to choose. Note that higher-level modules can be used as team assignments and lower-level modules as individual assignments.

Module Interfaces and Access Functions

In order for programmers to work independently, each facility module must have a well-defined interface. The interface to a module consists of all information that other programmers must know about the module in order to write their own modules. Interface descriptions consist of two parts:

- Prose descriptions of the underlying assumptions that user programs are allowed to make
- Descriptions of programming constructs that can be used in program source text

These programming constructs are programs called access functions. When the rest of the software needs to use a facility, it calls an access function provided by the appropriate facility module. The access function descriptions should include calling formats, parameter semantics, parameter limitations, the effects of calls on future calls, calls that are considered errors, and restrictions on call sequences (see Figure 4-4). In the tape-handler example, user programs call a tape-handler access function in order to write a record on a tape.

The information belonging in an interface must be chosen carefully. If enough information is not made available in the interface, the modules will not fit together smoothly. In the tape-handler example, this might happen if a particular user needs to know how much space remains on the tape, but the module interface does not include an access function to reveal this information. If too much information is provided, part of the module's secret is given away; programs using the facility will cease to operate correctly if the secret is changed. In the tape drive example, this might happen if the interface revealed the exact time required to write a record. If a user program used an algorithm based on this timing information, it would no longer work correctly if the tape driver were replaced by a faster model.

Module Specifications

Module design documentation consists primarily of specifications (i.e., precise statements of what the modules must do to be considered correct). Specifications serve as problem statements for programmers, leaving them free to choose appropriate module implementations. Such specifications are sometimes called *black-box* specifications, in fact, since they define only externally visible module behavior. There are three main types of module specifications: interface specifications for facility modules (see Figure 4-5), task specifications for control modules (see Figure 4-6), and usage specifications for module interconnections (see Figure 4-7). A discussion of each follows.

Address Storage Module
GET_NUMADDRESSES: Returns the number of addresses in the file
CREATE_ADDRESS (person-id):   Creates a new record in the internal
file and associates it with the identifier "person-id." Increases by 1
the number returned by GET_NUMADDRESSES
GET_STREET(person-id):   Returns the street name stored for the individual identified by person-id
SET_ZIPCODE(person-id, zipcode):   Stores a zipcode for person identified by person-id.

Input Device Module
READ_CARD: Reads and returns the next card from the card reader.

Input Format Module
SET_INFORMAT(format-code):   Determines the input format to be used
for all subsequent input actions, until called again with different
format-code
READ_RECORD: Calls READ_CARD (or a different input device program, depending on the device in use) to read in data; analyzes it into
records and fields; calls Address storage "SET" functions to store
the data for use by other programs.

Output Device Module
WRITE_LINE(string):   Writes out a line to a printer

Output Format Module
SET_OUTFORMAT: Determines the output format to be used for subsequent addresses
WRITE_RECORD(person-id):   Prints the address associated with
person-id with correct spacing and punctuation according to a specified format. Retrieves data to be printed from the Address Storage
Module.

Selection Module
SELECT_DOCTORS(person-id, is-doctor):   Returns a true/false indicator in "is-doctor" indicating whether the individual identified by
person-id is a doctor.

Command Module
INPUT_OPTION(format-code, medium-code):   Returns either the input
options selected by the user or the system defaults.

Figure 4-4. Some Access Functions of the Mailing List Example

Interface Specifications. Besides serving as problem statements, interface specifications communicate interface information to programmers of
other modules. These specifications serve as an agreement between the programmer of a module and the rest of the programmers, concerning what his
module will do. If his module meets its specifications, their modules should
work with it correctly. Programmers of the rest of the system should refer to
the interface specifications to find answers to their questions on the module. If
they cannot find a particular answer there, they should avoid making assumptions because information not documented in the interface specification

FUNCTION NAME: GET__STREET   MODULE: Address Storage
INPUT PARAMETERS:

Name	Type	Description
person-id	integer	identifier of an address

FUNCTION VALUE TYPE: Character string
FUNCTION VALUE: The street address stored for the address identi-
fied by person-id
EFFECT: None (i.e., no side effects)
ERROR ACTIONS: If person-id is not between 1 and
GET__NUMADDRESSES, then the module flags
UE__OUT__OF__RANGE; if the STREET field of the address
is undefined (i.e., SET__STREET has not been called for
"person-id"), then the module flags UE__UNDEFINED__FIELD.

FUNCTION NAME: READ__RECORD   MODULE: Input Format
INPUT PARAMETERS: None
FUNCTION VALUE TYPE: None
FUNCTION VALUE: None
EFFECT: This function cannot be called legally until
SET__INFORMAT and SET__INMEDIUM have been called.
Reads in next record on the input medium identified by
SET__INMEDIUM; analyzes it according to format identified by
SET__INFORMAT. After this program has been called, other pro-
grams can call Address Storage programs to read the component
values of the new record.
ERROR ACTIONS: If the assumed format does not match the record
format, then UE__WRONG__FORMAT is flagged by this mod-
ule.

Figure 4-5. Interface Specifications for the Mailing List Program Example

---

Master Control Module Specifications

Prerequisite data:
1. What type of action or actions to take (input, print, or both).
2. If action is to input new addresses, what input medium and format
   should be used.
3. If action is to print a mailing list, what print format and selection criteria
   should be used.

Requirements (i.e., what must be true after the system has run)
1. If any prerequisite data is missing, print error message.
2. If input is requested:
   • If the format is recognized as a legal format and it matches the in-
     put, then address data from the input file is subsequently retriev-
     able from the address storage module.
   • If the format is not recognized or does not match the input, then an
     error message is printed.
3. If output is requested:
   • If the print format and selection criteria are recognized as legal op-
     tions, then all addresses in the address storage module corres-
     ponding to the selection criteria are printed out according to the se-
     lected format.
   • If any options are not recognized, then an error message is printed.

Figure 4-6. Task Specifications for the Mailing List Program Example

should be part of the module secret. If they cannot write their programs with only the information in the interface specification, they must appeal to the designer to correct the interface. The requirement that users of a module refer only to module specifications is the principal means of limiting the amount of direct communication among programmers and of preventing the use of a module's secret by programmers of other modules.

Task Specifications. Task specifications for a control module define which part of the overall system requirements it must meet. These specifications can be written in terms of references to the overall system specification.

Usage Specifications. Usage specifications limit interconnections between modules by stating, for each program, which other programs it can call. These limitations are required so that the system is not so interrelated that no part of it works without all the rest of it available. Usage specifications also show the control structure of the overall program.

MASTER__CONTROL uses:	INPUT__OPTION	To find out user input format and medium choices
	READ__RECORD	To read in new records and put them in the file
	SELECT__DOCTORS	To find out for a particular address whether it should be printed in the doctors mailing list
	WRITE__RECORD	To print out a selected address
INPUT__OPTION uses:	READ__CARD	To read in a control card on the card reader
READ__RECORD uses:	READ__CARD	To read in a card image from the card reader
	CREATE__ADDRESS	To create a new address in the file
	SET__ZIPCODE	To store the zipcode field for that address
SELECT__DOCTORS uses:	GET__TITLE	To read the title field in an address to see if it equals "Dr." or "Doctor"
WRITE__RECORD uses:	GET__STREET	To get the street data that it is supposed to print
	WRITE__LINE	To write out a line on the line printer

Figure 4-7. Usage Specifications for the Mailing List Program Example

The concepts discussed thus far form the basis of modular programming. Designing and implementing modular programs can increase programmer productivity in the following ways:

- By producing program designs that are easier to code
- By producing programs that are easier to integrate
- By producing programs that are easier to modify
- By reducing the need for intra-project-team communication
- By reducing the amount of training required for those joining project teams midstream
- By requiring design documentation that helps maintenance programmers
- By producing reusable modules and designs

METHODOLOGY AND RELATED ISSUES

The steps of a methodology for dividing a system into modules and for writing module specifications are not strictly sequential: the products of one step need not be fully determined before the next step is started. Earlier steps can be iterated if working out details in the later steps reveals errors in the overall design.

The proper product of module design is documentation, not code. Module documentation has many uses during the life cycle of a program, including:

- Allowing the designer to communicate the design to reviewers
- Outlining work assignments for programmers
- Defining module interfaces, reducing interactions among programmers
- Guiding integrators as they put modules together and search for sources of errors
- Guiding maintenance programmers as they search for the right module to change or correct

Discussed in the following paragraphs is the appropriate documentation for each stage in the method. Questions that should be asked when reviewing the documentation are suggested.

MODULAR PROGRAM DESIGN METHODOLOGY

Step 1: Identify Secrets

Based on the system requirements, knowledge of the applications area, and experience with similar systems, the designer should list all aspects of the system that are likely to change. To supplement his own experience, the designer may want to interview the customers (users) to gain their ideas of future enhancements for the system, reference change request files for similar systems, and consult with other experienced designers. It is important to resist the notion that system requirements are fixed and unchangeable.

It is especially sensible to encapsulate any aspect of the system that is difficult to program correctly (e.g., scaled arithmetic on a fixed-point machine). If this is done, the error-prone operations are performed systematically throughout the system and are isolated in one module, where they can be programmed and debugged by a single expert.

Each *secret* that is identified in this step should be encapsulated in a separate module. In order to make the individual modules small and easy to understand, secrets should be identified in considerable detail. The system has been sufficiently decomposed when the work assignment represented by each module is small enough for one programmer to do it and small enough that it would be practical to throw it out and start over if the secret changed substantially.

Tables 4-1 and 4-2 list the types of secrets commonly found in DP and real-time systems. The lists are not all-inclusive.

The product of this design step is a detailed list of secrets and a corresponding list of small modules. The module descriptions should not refer to details that are the secrets of other modules. The documentation should be reviewed for completeness and consistency by people other than the designers. The primary review question of this step is: Are all plausible types of changes listed as module secrets? Potential users are often able to think of other changes when shown such a list.

Table 4-1. Common Secrets in Data Processing Systems

Secret	Typical Reasons for Changes
Data Base Structure (logical)	• New fields needed in records • Field sizes changed • More records required • Faster access required for particular fields
Algorithms	• Different time-space trade-offs required • More accurate or efficient algorithms invented
Data Storage (physical)	• Size of available storage changed • Type of available storage changed (e.g., from one tape drive model to another or from tape to disk) • Faster access required
Input	• Input medium changed (e.g., from cards to OCR) • Fields rearranged within records • More extensive error-checking required • Input sequence changed (e.g., from unsorted to sorted)
Output	• Change in output device (e.g., from printer to computer output microform)
Operating System Interface (e.g., JCL)	• New release issued by manufacturer
Software Functions as Seen by User	• New types of reports required • Changes in report formats required by client • New data added to input records

Table 4-2. Common Secrets in Real-Time Systems

Secret	Typical Change
Computer Characteristics	• Computer replaced by faster, larger, or cheaper model • Computer replaced by standard model (e.g., military standard)
Peripheral Devices	• Sensors replaced by more accurate, more reliable, or faster versions • Displays replaced by more flexible or more reliable models
Resource Allocation (e.g., scheduling)	• Relative priorities of activities changed • Single computer replaced by set of micro-computers • Capacity of resources changed (new memory)
Algorithms	• More accurate or faster algorithms invented • More general algorithm invented that can replace several more specialized algorithms
Software Functions	• User preferences changed, including: —New modes needed —Transition between modes changed —New responses required to user inputs —New displays needed • Computer-driven devices used for different purposes

Step 2: Devise the Module Hierarchy

Since any substantial system may have hundreds of small modules, people will find it difficult to understand the overall structure or to find the correct module to change unless the modules are organized into a comprehensible structure such as a module hierarchy. To design the module hierarchy, secrets and their corresponding modules are grouped into classes having something in common. For example, all modules that communicate with peripheral devices can be grouped into a single class. If there are more than 10 classes, the classes should be grouped into classes in the same way. There is no standard method for determining the correct class groupings; whatever makes the system easier to grasp is permissible if the designer is still free to make changes as he or she proceeds.

It is important that the structure accurately describe the software product: every secret must be accounted for somewhere in the structure, and it should be possible to locate every secret by starting at the top and working down. It is important that the designer develop clear criteria for class membership.

A good place to look for help in this step is the module hierarchy of a successful modular system that has similar functional requirements.

The product of this step is high-level program documentation, showing the top-level module classes and how each is broken down into successively smaller modules. The document should contain indexes and cross-references, including an alphabetized list of secrets with pointers to the associated module descriptions.

The module hierarchy should be independently reviewed for completeness and consistency. The following review questions should be asked:
- Are all important aspects of the system accounted for?
- Is it easy to find the module corresponding to a typical change request?
- Are the criteria for class membership clear?
- Are the module descriptions clear and unambiguous?

Step 3: Design Module Interfaces and Write Module Specifications

The next step is to design the module interfaces and to write black-box specifications for the externally visible behavior of each module. Because of the close relationship between these two activities, they are described as a single step.

Designing the interfaces properly is crucial for attaining the benefits of modularity. A module interface should not have to change when the module secret changes. For example, the interface to a sort module should not reveal the sort algorithm chosen so that the algorithm can be replaced by a faster algorithm without requiring the access function calls in the user programs to change.

To design the interface to a particular module, the designer should first list all the assumptions he or she is willing to allow other programmers to make about it. The following are examples of typical assumptions:
- It is assumed that the input list is already sorted.
- It is assumed that all tape drivers will rewind tapes.
- It is assumed that all mailing addresses will include name, street, city, and state data.

It should be noted that if these assumptions change, user programs that depend on them will have to change.

Assumptions are usually documented in prose so that they can be reviewed by programmers and nonprogrammers familiar with the application area. For example, the set of assumptions that user programs are allowed to make about the tape handler module should be reviewed by those familiar with tape driver devices. Review questions might be:
- Are the assumptions true of the current device?
- Are they true of replacement devices on the market?
- Are they true of replacement devices being developed?

The list of assumptions should also be reviewed by programmers, who should determine what choices are eliminated by the assumptions and whether these choices might be desirable alternatives.

Once the assumptions have been listed and reviewed, specifications for the access functions are written. Access functions incorporate the assumptions in a form that can be used in programs. Access functions should be specified rigorously in terms of externally visible behavior. Questions to be answered for each function include:

- What parameters does it require? In what order? What are the restrictions on legal parameter values? What do the parameters mean?
- What effect does calling this function have on future calls to access functions belonging to this module?
- What errors can be associated with this access function? What action is to be taken in each case?

Additional questions to be answered in the specifications include:

- Does the module have to be initialized? How? What happens if it is not initialized?
- What information or facilities does the module require from other programs for it to operate correctly?
- What are the time and space budgets for this module?

The access function specifications should be reviewed thoroughly by senior programmers. The review should consist of three parts:

- A cross-check against the assumptions—Is all information in the assumptions accounted for by at least one access function? Are any additional assumptions made? (If so, these assumptions should be written out and reviewed.)
- Implementation feasibility—Can the access functions be implemented with reasonable efficiency?
- Effects on other programs—Can user programs be written reasonably efficiently with calls to these access functions? Can they get their own jobs done?

Task specifications must be written in terms of the overall system requirements. Writing task specifications is much easier if the system requirements are properly documented because they can consist mainly of references to the requirements documentation. These specifications do not include access function descriptions because control modules have no access functions.

In the process of writing module specifications, the designer makes many design decisions. These issues should be documented as should the alternatives that are considered and the reasons for making a particular choice. Difficult decisions are not really made until they are written down; people continue to discuss design problems until there is some record of their resolution. This type of documentation provides invaluable guidance to maintenance programmers, who consider the same issues when they evaluate the feasibility of requested changes. Documenting design issues not only makes systems easier to maintain but helps train programmers to become designers by exposing them to the factors that influence design.

Step 4: Write the Usage Specifications

While designing the interconnections between programs, the designer should seek to avoid two expensive errors: unnecessary code duplication and interdependencies. If there is already a module to provide a facility, it is wasteful of programmer time and computer space for other programmers to write their own code to implement the same facility. If they do, the final system will have sections of code that are similar but not quite the same, making the maintenance programmer's job more difficult. Interdependencies, which exist when two programs use each other either directly or indirectly, make the system difficult to integrate, test, and maintain. For example, if an operating system scheduler module depends on the file system to maintain its data and the file system depends on the scheduler to schedule its disk accesses, neither component can work unless the other is present and working. Thus, neither component can be tested without the other, making incremental integration impossible. In addition, neither component can be reused in another system without the other (e.g., the scheduler module could not be reused in a simpler operating system without disk storage).

To write the usage specifications, the designer must list the legal interconnections, trying to avoid both problems mentioned previously. This compromise can be characterized as avoiding loops in the uses relation [3]. The best way to start is by listing all programs that will not be allowed to use any other programs; these programs form the bottom level of a hierarchy. Next, all programs that use only programs in the layer should be listed below; these form the next level. This process continues, with the programs at each level using only programs in the lower levels.

Documentation for this step should include a list for each program, showing the programs it can use. In addition, there should be lists of programs at each level. These lists can be used to plan system integration; the bottom level can be tested first, then the next level added and tested, and so on.

PERFORMANCE ISSUES

Modular programming can increase the memory or execution time required for a particular program. If this happens, software managers must consider a basic trade-off: if the modular program is easier to understand, modify, and test than is an unmodular counterpart, is modular design worth a small performance cost (especially since hardware costs are decreasing and programmer salaries increasing)?

There are two main sources of performance penalties in modular programs: increased context switching, caused by additional subroutine calls, and the requirement of more operations, caused by separating the program into different modules. If a project has no performance leeway at all, there are certain actions that can be taken to speed up and slim down a modular program.

More Context Switching

If every access function in a module is a subroutine, modular programming can result in substantially more subroutine calls than with nonmodular programming. Consider the mailing list system described earlier. The Address Storage module interface provides an access function, GET_STREET(person-id) that returns the street address of the individual identified by person-id. If the programmer who implements the module decides to store the street addresses in an array in which each array element is a PL/1-type structure containing all data associated with a particular person, a call to the access function GET_STREET becomes an array reference, ADDRESS__DATA(person-id).STREET. If the user were permitted to know the secret of the module and to access the array directly, a subroutine call could be avoided, and the program would run slightly faster. In this case, however, if it were decided to replace the array with a linked list, it would be necessary to change every program that accessed the data, not just the single access function.

This problem can be avoided by implementing some of the access functions as macros. With macros, the secret of the module is hidden from other programs without any additional run-time context switching. If GET__STREET were implemented as a macro, during macro expansion all calls to it would be replaced by the appropriate array reference. The advantages of modularity would be preserved because programmers look at the source text, not the expanded code. Many high-order programming languages provide macro facilities that can be used in this way.

More Operations

Separating independently changeable concerns into different modules can result in an increased number of operations because programmers are not allowed to fold together operations too tightly. In a real-time system with one module that hides sensor characteristics and one that hides the details of filtering algorithms, programs in the sensor module must take the following steps:

1. Read in raw values from the sensor and scale them for compatibility with the engineering units expected by other programs.
2. Apply a correction for a known bias.
3. Call a filter access function to smooth out fluctuations.

If the programmer were allowed to write his own filter algorithm, he or she might be able to combine some of the arithmetic operations of the filtering with the operations required to scale and correct the value. Of course, separating the algorithms into different modules has major advantages: a maintenance programmer can change the sensor correction without having to understand the filter or untangle the algebraic combination of the two algorithms. This can, however, result in increased execution time, even if the filter program is a macro, so that there is no run-time context switching. The authors of this chapter know no cure for this problem.

Tuning a Modular Program

It is well known that programs usually spend most of their execution time in relatively small portions of the code, often called bottlenecks. Because there are usually only a few bottlenecks, where extra subroutine calls or extra operations incur a significant speed penalty, a small number of program modifications can lead to major improvements. After a system is integrated, its performance can be measured in order to find the bottlenecks. The modular structure makes it easy to make the changes that result in a considerable improvement: algorithms and data structures are isolated so that it is easy to replace them with faster or smaller choices without massive reprogramming.

MANAGEMENT CONSIDERATIONS

Project Scheduling. Properly modularized software is easier and less expensive to code, integrate, alter, and maintain. It can, however, be more difficult and time-consuming to design. An early investment in careful design can pay off over the rest of the software life cycle, but it can also cause a considerable amount of money to be spent before there is any running code. Managers who measure productivity in terms of lines of code can find this disturbing, but it is a mistake to pressure the software team to start coding before the design is complete. Such shortsightedness can be very expensive in the long run because it compromises the simplicity and integrity of the software design. It is important that managers and customers be aware that initial costs are necessary so that they do not conclude prematurely that modular programming is a detriment rather than a help.

Personnel. Software system designers should be able to express their design concepts in clear, precise terms. The product is more likely to be coherent and cleanly designed if a small number of experienced people design it than if the whole programming team has a part in it. F. P. Brooks calls his decision to have 150 rather than 10 people design OS/360 "a multimillion dollar mistake" [4], for exactly this reason.

Designers should also have access to people who can review their documentation from several viewpoints. Some reviewers should be familiar with the application: these people look for gaps, misunderstandings about the requirements, and assumptions that are likely to change. Other reviewers should be expert programmers: they look for modules that will be difficult to implement and design decisions that will result in inefficient programs.

Documentation Support. Sufficient secretarial and WP support must be provided to keep documentation up-to-date. Procedures must be established to make and distribute documentation changes reflecting design changes. These procedures should be, on the one hand, carefully controlled so that changes are not haphazardly introduced and, on the other hand, sufficiently flexible that the software team is not hampered by excessive red tape.

Note:

The opinions expressed in this chapter are those of the authors. The chapter is not endorsed by the U.S. Government and does not represent an official U.S. Government position. The authors are grateful to their colleagues at the Naval Research Laboratory for the stimulating discussions that contributed to their understanding of the techniques. They are particularly grateful to David Parnas, whose contributions to the field of software engineering form the basis of much that appears in this chapter. They are also grateful to Edward Britton and David Parnas for reviewing the manuscript.

References

1. Brooks, F.P., Jr. *The Mythical Man-Month: Essays on Software Engineering.* Reading MA: Addison-Wesley, 1975.
2. Parnas, D. "On the Criteria to be Used in Decomposing Systems into Modules." *Communications of the ACM.* Vol. 15, No. 12. (December 1972).
3. Parnas, D. "Designing Software for Ease of Extension and Contraction." *IEEE Transactions on Software Engineering.* SE-5(2), March 1979.
4. Brooks, F.P., Jr. *The Mythical Man-Month: Essays on Software Engineering.* Reading MA: Addison-Wesley, 1975.

5 Decision Tables

by Paul F. Barbuto, Jr.

INTRODUCTION

Decision tables, a powerful technique that can be applied to the solution of computing problems, are compatible with top-down design, programming, and testing. They function in a number of areas: analysis, design, programming, and documentation. Because they are so useful and so often ignored, decision tables qualify for the title of structured programming's forgotten technique.

Designing with decision tables is no different than other styles of designing except that the result is more spatially organized. The decision table structure facilitates a top-down design where the control structure is expressed in the table and the "pure code" exists in the action stubs. The decision to produce more than one such table as part of a design effort is similar to that made to introduce another level in any other hierarchical design. Normally, decision tables would represent a node of the hierarchy or a subtree (the part of the hierarchy beneath a node). Partitioning the design into tables is motivated by the usual considerations of program size and homogeneity of purpose. For example, a small program might be represented by two decision tables: one for normal processing and error determination and a second table to sort out and process the error conditions.

Because decision tables communicate logic clearly, they can be considered documentation tools. In the design stage, the specifications easily motivate (can be transformed into) a preliminary table that can be verified with the user. The table, then, becomes part of the documentation. The same table can be translated from the symbolic "read input" to the actual read statement in a chosen implementation language, and if a decision table translator is available, the decision table can be a vehicle that literally takes the idea from inception through implementation and testing.

It is easy to include probes to collect testing coverage information in a decision table implementation; this assists in evaluating the quality of program testing.

Resistance to using decision tables seems unfounded; it is primarily attributable to lack of knowledge. Although decision tables are laid out spatially, they require no more skills to use than do other programming aids. Decision tables make linear translation unnecessary, since they replace linear representation with a multidimensional representation of the solution to the problem. In the case of machine translation, one additional piece of system software needs to be supported; however, if resistance to supporting system software were a valid point, one would be writing in machine language.

DESCRIPTION AND DEFINITION

Decision tables are sometimes referred to more precisely as *decision logic tables*. Each word contributes precision to the definition.

Decision relates to the making of choices.

Logic relates to making the choices in a logical fashion by using current conditions to determine the future course of action.

Tables relates to the manner in which the relationship between extant conditions and future actions are recorded. The rules relating conditions to actions are represented in tabular form.

The process of understanding, reading, interpreting, or executing a decision table depends on selecting the appropriate rule from the table (based on an evaluation of current conditions) and performing the indicated actions.

Anatomy of a Decision Table

The anatomy of a decision table is shown in Figure 5-1. Its four primary parts can be characterized by two dichotomies: conditions versus actions and stubs versus entries.

Table Name	Stubs	Entries
Conditions	Condition Stubs	Condition Entries
Actions	Action Stubs	Action Entries

Figure 5-1. Anatomy of a Decision Table

Conditions versus actions divides the decision table parts according to the conditions (data) existing when the table is entered and the inputs (what is observed) as well as the actions taken as the result of the inputs, or that might be taken, given a different set of input conditions (what is done). Stubs versus entries distinguishes between the stub that contains the question or action to take and the entries that represent answers to the question or indications that a particular action is to be taken. Thus, the four main parts of a decision table, as shown in Figure 5-1, are:

- Condition stubs—questions that can be used to determine the state of the process or program on entry to the table.
- Condition entries—the sets of answers to the condition stub questions, each set representing a possible state of the process or program. The answers to the questions are arranged vertically, and each column identifies a different course of action or policy (a rule).
- Action stubs—an ordered list of actions (a menu) from which a set of actions is selected.
- Action entries—the selection list (from the action stubs) that relates a set of actions to be performed to a given input state. It is coded at the bottom of each rule.

Another important part of the decision table is the table name, which is useful for referencing the table (e.g., execute table input edit). A sample decision table (shown in Figure 5-2) might involve one's policy concerning wearing a raincoat when leaving for work:

"If it rains, I put on a raincoat before I go to work."

One enters the table in the upper left-hand corner, asking the question, "Is it raining?" One evaluates the answer in the upper right-hand corner, choosing the "Rain Rule" or "Dry Rule," depending upon the answer to the question. One then proceeds down the chosen rule (column) and looks for an "X" that shows that the listed action should be done. In the Rain Rule, one first puts on a raincoat and then leaves for work. In the Dry Rule, after deciding it is not raining, one leaves for work.

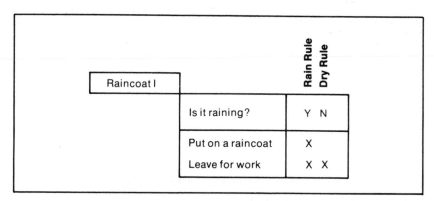

Figure 5-2. Raincoat Decision Table I

If one decided to wear a raincoat, if rain were predicted, the decision table would be revised, as shown in Figure 5-3. A comparison of the rules in Figures 5-2 and 5-3 shows that for the first three, the actions taken (outcomes) are the same. If the conventional notation of a dash (—) is used to indicate "Do Not

Care," two alternate but equivalent decision tables can be produced (see Figures 5-4 and 5-5). They differ with respect to which condition is ignored when two rules with similar actions are collapsed. There is no required order among the conditions or rules.

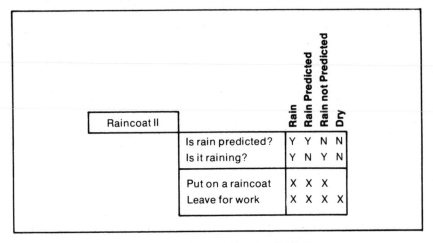

Figure 5-3. Raincoat Decision Table II

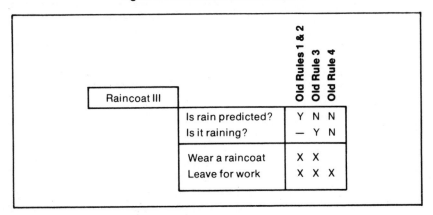

Figure 5-4. Raincoat Decision Table III

The decision table in Figure 5-6 also represents the raincoat-wearing policy. Note that two rules can be interchanged and two conditions can be interchanged. Although one of the equivalent tables may be preferable, based on a specific view of the problem, the decision tables shown in Figures 5-3 through 5-6 are all equivalent. It is frequently helpful to view alternative representations of the captured policies presented in a decision table.

There is, however, a canonical form for decision tables. Figures 5-3 and 5-4 are in canonical form; Figures 5-5 and 5-6 are not. To place a decision table in canonical form:

1. The conditions must be sorted into ascending order with respect to the number of Do Not Care responses. Within groups of conditions with the same number of Do Not Cares, the conditions must be sorted into ascending order with respect to the number of N responses. This tends to put conditions with the most positive ''information'' near the top of the decision table.
2. The rules must be sorted, placing Do Not Cares before Ys and Ys before Ns, treating the first row as a high-ordered position, and so on, down to the last condition specified (see Figure 5-3).

Figure 5-5 violates the first sort on conditions; the Do Not Cares should have been in the second row. Figure 5-6 violates the second sort; the second and third rules must be interchanged.

Although having decision tables in canonical form is not truly necessary, they are often more tractable. Fortunately, this can easily be done automatically (this is discussed later in this chapter).

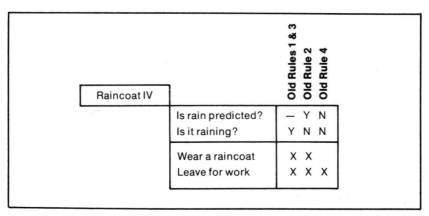

Raincoat IV	Old Rules 1 & 3	Old Rule 2	Old Rule 4
Is rain predicted?	—	Y	N
Is it raining?	Y	N	N
Wear a raincoat	X	X	
Leave for work	X	X	X

Figure 5-5. Raincoat Decision Table IV

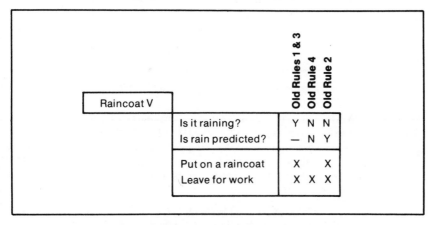

Raincoat V	Old Rules 1 & 3	Old Rule 4	Old Rule 2
Is it raining?	Y	N	N
Is rain predicted?	—	N	Y
Put on a raincoat	X		X
Leave for work	X	X	X

Figure 5-6. Raincoat Decision Table V

COMMON CONTROL STRUCTURES

The common control structures of structured programming can be compared with decision tables.

The IF THEN ELSE control structure is displayed as a flowchart in Figure 5-7 and as a decision table in Figure 5-8. Just as $X = B$ or $X = C$ in the example could be replaced in structured programming by any other single-entry, single-exit block of code, the same type of substitution could be made in the decision table.

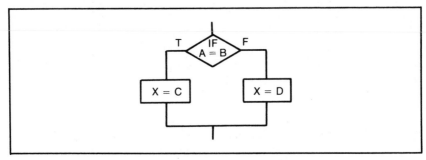

Figure 5-7. IF THEN ELSE Flowchart

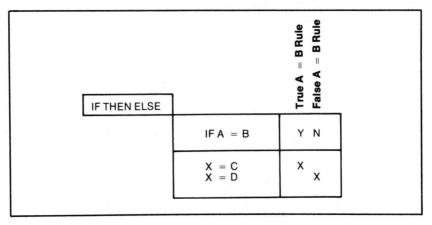

Figure 5-8. IF THEN ELSE Decision Table

The DO WHILE structure is shown as a flowchart in Figure 5-9 and as a decision table in Figure 5-10. As with IF THEN ELSE, the simple statements could be replaced with more complex single-entry, single-exit structures. It should be noted how the condition to be tested is separated from the actions to be taken and how clearly the alternative courses of actions are identified and related to the input conditions.

The CASE STATEMENT is displayed in Figure 5-11 as a flowchart and in Figure 5-12 as a decision table. While it would be possible to default if X were not equal to one or two, that is, to assume X is equal to three, decision tables lend themselves to the more logically complete expression; if none of the above, then it is an error, as demonstrated in the fourth rule.

The following example combines control structures:

> **Problem:** Read in a deck of cards, sum together data from alternate cards, and print out the two sums and number of cards read.

Figure 5-13 shows a decision table describing the process; developing the equivalent flowchart is left to the reader.

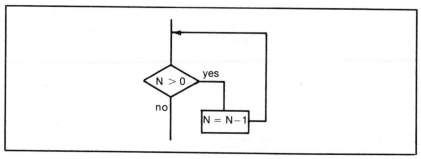

Figure 5-9. DO WHILE Flowchart

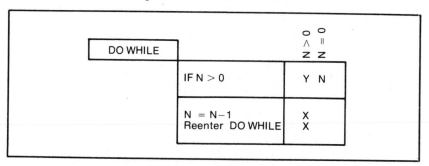

Figure 5-10. DO WHILE Decision Table

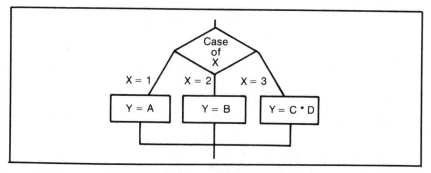

Figure 5-11. CASE STATEMENT Flowchart

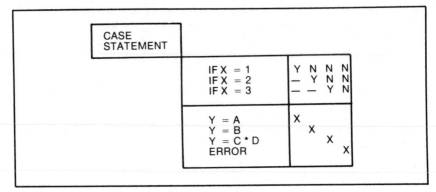

Figure 5-12. CASE STATEMENT Decision Table

ALTERNATE SUMS	STARTUP	EOF	EVEN CARD	ODD CARD
STARTUP	Y	N	N	N
EOF	–	Y	N	N
#_READ_TRIES IS EVEN	–	–	Y	N
#_READ_TRIES=0	X			
EVEN, ODD=0	X			
EVEN=EVEN+X			X	
ODD=ODD+X				X
#_READ_TRIES= #_READ_TRIES+1	X		X	X
READ X	X		X	X
STARTUP=N	X			
REENTER ALTERNATE SUMS	X		X	X
#_CARDS=#_READ_TRIES−1		X		
PRINT #_CARDS, EVEN, ODD		X		

Note: STARTUP must be set equal to YES before entering table for the first time.

Figure 5-13. ALTERNATE SUMS Decision Table

Limited versus Extended Entries

The types of decision tables discussed so far are called limited-entry decision tables. They are limited in that their condition entries are only Yes, No, or Do Not Care (−), and the action entries are Do It, X or Do Not Do It, and blank. Extended-entry tables admit a wider variety of entries, much as a CASE STATEMENT permits more states than an IF THEN ELSE statement. Examples of condition stubs and condition entries are:

- $X = 1,2,3,4,5$
- Condition stubs querying the relationship A : B
- Condition entries specifying the relationship $< = >$, $>$, $<$, and the like

Similarly, Action Stub $Y =$, with Action Entries 1, 2, 3, 4, 5 in different rules, is permitted in extended-entry decision tables. Although these appear more powerful, they are not; in fact, anything that can be expressed as an extended entry can be expressed as a combination of limited-entry conditions or actions. Such recoding is shown in Figures 5-14 and 5-15 and in Figures 5-16 and 5-17. The rest of this discussion, therefore, is restricted to limited-entry decision tables, without loss of generality.

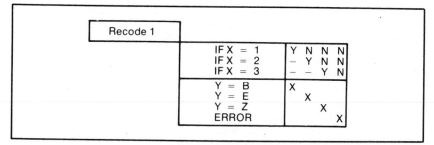

Figure 5-14. Extended Example 1

Recode 1				
IF X = 1	Y	N	N	N
IF X = 2	–	Y	N	N
IF X = 3	–	–	Y	N
Y = B	X			
Y = E		X		
Y = Z			X	
ERROR				X

Figure 5-15. Recode 1

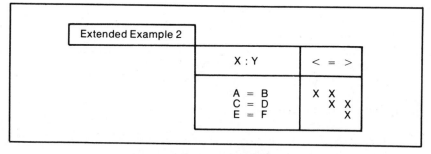

Figure 5-16. Extended Example 2

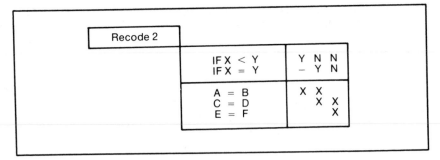

Figure 5-17. Recode 2

Decision Table Properties

Several properties of decision tables make them effective vehicles for capturing the design process: completeness, unambiguousness, limited paths, and usefulness in debugging and testing.

Completeness. It is possible to determine mathematically whether a limited-entry decision table represents all possible outcomes implied in the given situation. Only one rule should apply. In a limited-entry decision table with two conditions, there are a maximum of 2 times 2, or 4 rules; with three conditions, 2 times 2 times 2, or 8 rules; 4 conditions, 16 rules; n conditions, 2^n rules. This does not mean that each decision table with five conditions must have 32 rules, although it might, if each possible co-occurrence of input conditions elicited a different set of actions (responses). In most cases, some conditions are more important than others, so if a certain condition occurs, the others can be ignored. The technique for counting rules when testing the decision table for completeness must therefore take Do Not Care conditions into account. Specifically, in thinking about what the Do Not Care dash indicates, it can be concluded that a rule with one dash represents the rule with a Y as well as the rule with an N in that position. Thus, a single dash in a rule counts as two. A rule with two dashes represents 2^2 rules (the rule with (Y,Y), (Y,N), (N,Y) and (N,N) substituted for the two dashes). The number of rules that a rule with Do Not Care dashes has is equal to 2^n, when n is the number of dashes. This sum is equal to 2^x, where x is the number of conditions, if the table is complete, provided the rules are unambiguous (as defined in the next section).

Examples of two decision tables are shown in Figures 5-18 and 5-19. Figure 5-18 is missing two rules. The two rules marked with asterisks in Figure 5-19 represent those that are missing from Figure 5-18. They could have been accidentally forgotten, logically impossible, or impossible according to the specifications. In any case, they probably deserve at least an action: "Error should never have occurred." Some designers define an ELSE RULE to pick up missed rules; however, the practice weakens this analysis and should be avoided.

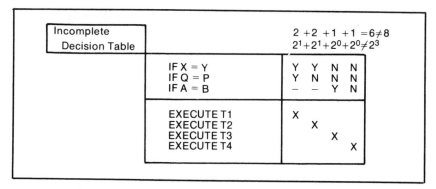

Incomplete Decision Table	$2 +2 +1 +1 =6 \neq 8$ $2^1+2^1+2^0+2^0 \neq 2^3$			
IF X = Y	Y	Y	N	N
IF Q = P	Y	N	N	N
IF A = B	−	−	Y	N
EXECUTE T1	X			
EXECUTE T2		X		
EXECUTE T3			X	
EXECUTE T4				X

Figure 5-18. Incomplete Decision Table

Completed XQA Decision Table	$2 +2 +1 +1 +1 +1 =8$ $2^1+2^1+2^0+2^0+2^0+2^0=2^3$ * *					
IF X = Y	Y	Y	N	N	N	N
IF Q = P	Y	N	Y	Y	N	N
IF A = B	−	−	Y	N	Y	N
EXECUTE T1	X					
EXECUTE T2		X				
EXECUTE T3					X	
EXECUTE T4						X
ERROR			X	X		

Note:
* Missing from Figure 5-18

Figure 5-19. Completed Version of Figure 5-18

The property of completeness and the straightforward means of evaluating it are important as an analysis, design, and programming aid. It permits (or forces) consideration of whether all possible eventualities have been planned for, given the set of conditions to be tested. In a regular, linearly written program, it is not evident what co-occurrences of conditions are considered. Perhaps no one has thought of all possible co-occurrences.

Unambiguousness. Rules must be unambiguous when being counted; they are considered so if they are mutually exclusive and exhaustive. This means that no two rules apply at the same time. Functionally, this requires that rules be distinguishable from each other. This means that any two rules must differ with respect to YN on at least one condition: $(Y,-)$, $(N,-)$, (Y,Y), (N,N), $(-,Y)$, or $(-,N)$ do not. The only two that differ are (Y,N) and (N,Y). Although checking decision tables for ambiguity takes time—to examine each pair of rules (for n rules, $n*(n-1)/2$ pairs)—the assurance that only one rule applies makes the effort worthwhile.

Checking for completeness and mutual exclusivity is a valuable evaluation tool. This well-defined checking process can easily be relegated to a computer.

Limited Paths. The analysis to evaluate nonambiguity and completeness demonstrates the limited number of paths within a decision table. Thus, given the conditions being tested, their logical impact has been completely evaluated. There is no other way in which they can co-occur, and all of the ways identified are explicitly listed side by side. It is then possible to compare actions taken under different rules or to identify under which rules a given action occurs. It is often possible to assign names to rules; for example, "start up," "wrap up," "normal loop," and "new type." This naming aids in evaluating the proposed design, and knowing all paths is relevant in terms of debugging.

Debugging and Testing. As Chapter 10 will indicate, important aspects of testing include evaluating the coverage of testing and determining sequences of flow groups. Rules conveniently represent flow groups so that coverage and flow group sequence can be examined using the rule as a unit of measure. For example, in testing, have all the rules been exercised? Have all possible sequences occurred?

The point in the decision table implementation where the rule has been identified, and before any actions for that rule have been taken, is a practical place to log which rule has been identified and the sequential (pairwise) rule transitions. It is quite simple to include this feature in machine translation.

MODIFICATION OF EXISTING TABLES

Modifications of decision tables are important in system development; one often starts with a simplified version of a table and revises it. Modifications are also important in the maintenance of existing programs, particularly since maintenance costs can be more than 50 percent in the software life cycle.

There are four basic ways in which a decision table can be changed:
• Change the number of rules.
• Change the number of conditions.
• Change the number of actions.
• Reorder the actions.

Change the Number of Rules. The number of rules in a decision table can be changed without changing the number of conditions, while maintaining a complete, unambiguous set of rules, only by introducing or eliminating a Do Not Care. Doing this would decrease or increase the number of rules; for example, Figure 5-20 would become like Figure 5-21, or Figure 5-21 would become like Figure 5-20 if a rule were added or deleted, respectively. This type of change occurs when there is no need to distinguish between two rules because the actions are the same or when a slight clarification of a particular rule definition is necessary. Usually, in the clarification or simplification process, when the number of rules changes, so does the number of conditions.

Change the Number of Conditions. The number of conditions changes when it is determined (during analysis) that a question has become superfluous or that an additional question must be asked to prescribe a solution correctly.

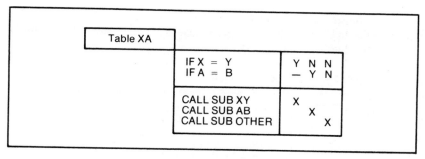

Figure 5-20. Decision Table XA

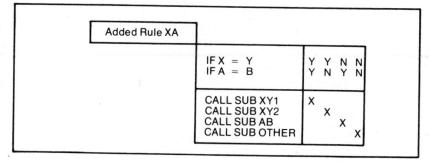

Figure 5-21. Decision Table XA with Rule Added

The deletion of a condition occurs when all of the condition entries for the specified condition have become Do Not Cares because of two rules collapsing into one. For example, when the condition A = B becomes superfluous, the decision table in Figure 5-20 becomes like that shown in Figure 5-22.

Deleted Condition XA

IF X = Y	Y	N
IF A = B	—	—
CALL SUB XY	X	
CALL SUB OTHER		X

Figure 5-22. Decision Table XA: Superfluous Condition

Sometimes, however, a condition is missing from the original decision table. Unless the condition is being added specifically to clarify (divide) a specific rule, it can be useful to double the number of rules (splitting each from the original table into two rules). The set of actions from the original rule can be duplicated and, after evaluating the suitability of the rules and revising them as necessary, the pair of rules that have identical actions can be collapsed. For example, after the addition of IF C = D and the prescribed expansion, the decision table in Figure 5-20 becomes like that shown in Figure 5-23. Figure 5-24 represents the revised table after manual intervention because of a logical process external to the decision table. After collapsing the rules with identical actions, Figure 5-24 becomes like Figure 5-25.

Added Condition XA	Old Rule Numbers { 1 1 2 2 3 3
IF X = Y	Y Y N N N N
IF A = B	– – Y Y N N
IF C = D	Y N Y N Y N
CALL SUB XY	X X
CALL SUB AB	X X
CALL SUB OTHER	X X

Figure 5-23. Decision Table XA: Added Condition

Revised XA	New Rule Numbers { 1 2 3 4 5 6
	Old Rule Numbers { 1 1 2 2 3 3
IF X = Y	Y Y N N N N
IF A = B	– – Y Y N N
IF C = D	Y N Y N Y N
CALL SUB XY	X
CALL SUB AB	X
CALL SUB OTHER	X X X X

Figure 5-24. Decision Table XA: Revised

Collapsed XA	Old Rule Numbers { 1 2 3 4 5 6
IF X = Y	Y Y N N N
IF A = B	– – Y Y N
IF C = D	Y N Y N –
CALL SUB XY	X
CALL SUB AB	X
CALL SUB OTHER	X X X

Figure 5-25. Decision Table XA: Collapsed

Change the Number of Actions. Adding an action is simple. The new action is entered in the list of action stubs, and appropriate entries are made in the action entries.

Reorder Actions in a Table. Obviously, actions can be reordered to modify the meaning of a table. They can also be reordered such that the meaning of the table is unchanged or that, at most, only the meanings of a few rules are changed. Once a rule is identified as the appropriate rule in that instance, the action entries for that rule are scanned, and, if indicated, a particular action stub is executed. Thus, within a rule, any action can be moved toward the top or bottom of the table, any distance from its original position, provided it is not moved beyond another action whose execution depends on its original position in the rule.

The range through which an action can be moved without changing the table's meaning is limited by the smallest move with respect to each rule in which it participates. In Figure 5-26, for example, with respect to Rule 1, the action $A = A - 1$ could be moved as far forward (toward the top of the table) as after $C = C - 1$ or as far backward as just before $D = D/2$ without changing the meaning of the first rule. Similarly, with respect to Rule 3, $A = A - 1$ could be moved forward as far as after $D = D + 1$, but it could not be moved backward from its present position. With respect to Rules 2 and 4, it could be moved anywhere in the lists of actions.

When the ranges are combined by looking for those most restricted, $A = A - 1$ can be moved forward, behind $C = C - 1$, but it cannot be moved backward without changing the original definition of the table. The point of this discussion is that these limitations represent a partial ordering of the actions, in which actions may be moved without modifying the meaning of the table. It should be understood, however, that it is often possible (with malice) to modify (reorder) one rule without modifying another by using this property. For instance, PRINT A could be moved before the action $A = A - 1$, changing the meaning of Rule 3 without changing the meaning of Rules 1, 2, and 4.

Only rarely is it necessary to duplicate an action to allow optimum ordering, as determined by the logic of the situation. This is usually unnecessary, however, because most actions are independent of each other and can thus be reordered without affecting the computation.

Reorder Table					
IF A = B	Y	Y	N	N
IF C = D	Y	N	Y	N
D = D+1		X		
C = C−1	X			
A = 2πD		X		X
A = A−1	X	X		
PRINT A		X	X	
B = B + 1				X
D = D / 2	X			

Figure 5-26. Reordering a Table

DECISION TABLES AS A SYSTEMS ANALYSIS TOOL

In exploring how to design using decision tables and how to do iterations on the design, the problem of designing a merge program can be considered.

The conditions would be identified as:
1. A KEY < B KEY
2. A KEY = B KEY
3. A KEY > B KEY

The actions to be performed would be identified as:
1. WRITE an output record from A File
2. READ a record from A File
3. WRITE an output record from B File Record
4. READ a record from B File

A preliminary decision table to merge the two files is shown in Figure 5-27. The decision table assumes that a record has been read from both files before the table is entered. The table, as defined, is an infinite process, and the specifications include an ambiguity. "Merge Files A and B" does not specify which record is to be placed in the output file first if equal keys are found.

To take care of the end-of-file condition, two new conditions, End of File A and End of File B, must be introduced; a new action, End of Job, is also required to show successful completion (see Figure 5-28). The precondition to entering the table is reduced to an attempted read of both files. Please observe that the original decision table (in Figure 5-27) is the same as Rules 4, 5, and 6 in Figure 5-28, where both End-of-File tests fail. It is frequently easier to develop a decision table to process the normal case and then expand it to take care of end cases, as has been done here. It can be seen, for instance, that even with one or both files empty, the revised table works. Notice also the action similarities between Rule 2 and Rule 6: Rule 2, End of File on File A Rule is similar to Rule 6, A KEY > B KEY. Likewise, Rule 3 parallels Rule 4. Neither pair can be collapsed, as their condition entries differ by more than one YN pair.

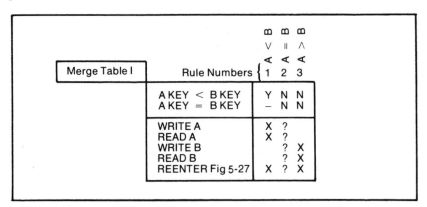

Figure 5-27. Preliminary Decision Table

Merge Table II	Rule Numbers	EOJ (1)	E of A (2)	E of B (3)	A < B (4)	A = B (5)	A > B (6)
EOFA		Y	Y	N	N	N	N
EOFB		Y	N	Y	N	N	N
A < B		–	–	–	Y	N	N
A = B		–	–	–	–	Y	N
WRITE A				X	X	?	
READ A				X	X	?	
WRITE B			X			?	X
READ B			X			?	X
LOOP			X	X	X	?	X
EOJ		X				?	

Merge Files A and B

Note: Before entering table, read Files A and B once.

Figure 5-28. Merging Files A and B: Table II

How to handle the A KEY = B KEY Case (Rule 5) must still be determined. One rejects writing and reading both files, since there might be multiple equal keys on one of the other files. Temporarily, records with equal keys from File A can be placed before records with equal keys from File B. This results in the decision table shown in Figure 5-29. Note the similarity in the actions for Rules 3, 4, and 5. It is possible to process File A and retain the status quo of File B in all three rules.

Merge Table III	Rule Numbers	EOJ (1)	E of A (2)	E of B (3)	A < B (4)	A = B (5)	A > B (6)
EOFA		Y	Y	N	N	N	N
EOFB		Y	N	Y	N	N	N
A < B		–	–	–	Y	N	N
A = B		–	–	–	–	Y	N
WRITE A				X	X	X	
READ A				X	X	X	
WRITE B			X				X
READ B			X				X
LOOP			X	X	X	X	X
EOJ		X					

Merge Files A and B.
Put equal As before Bs.

Note: Attempt read Files A and B once before entering table.

Figure 5-29. Merging Files A and B: Table III

Single versus Multiple Tables

Size and homogeneity of purpose are two factors that influence the use of multiple decision tables instead of one. Determining whether a decision table is too big depends more on the number of rules than on the number of conditions. At about the time the table becomes difficult to fit on one page (generally, more than 60 rules), groups of rules are likely to be forming. This clumping is often obvious logically or visually if the table is in canonical form. Other indicators of clumping would be that certain conditions are used in only a subset of rules. When a table is entered at a lower level of the hierarchy, it inherits the conditions of the rules that cause it to be executed. For example, a 60-rule table was used to implement a complicated three-way merge with date-matching of multiple records. Although it might have been possible to split the table, it was more advantageous to have the entire control structure in one place for perusal and sight verification. This is achieved by comparing logically similar rules (do they or should they have the same or similar actions?) and by viewing the actions one by one, comparing the rules that execute each action. One part of the process focuses on the columns of the table, the other on the rows. This type of analysis is difficult, if not impossible, in a linearly described design.

Transfer of Control in Multiple Decision Tables

A decision table as a whole can be executed in three basic ways:
- Sequentially
- As a subroutine (Execute, Perform, Call Return)
- By transfer of control (GO TO)

If a decision table is viewed as a rather complex CASE STATEMENT, it functions nicely as a structured construct. One can usually either flow through it sequentially (as with any other structured construct) or execute it with the assumption that the flow of control would return from it as it would from a subroutine.

Transfer of control without expecting a return is an alternative technique that is less compatible with a structured viewpoint. It is compatible if the GO TO statement specifies reentry into the same table, since transfer to itself is structurally equivalent to a CASE STATEMENT within a DO WHILE. This is the natural way to specify looping in a decision table; however, at least one rule must not reenter the table to provide a terminating condition for the loop, or an infinite loop will occur.

Any action containing a GO TO (reenter) should be at or near the bottom of the list of actions; it must be the last action in any rule in which it is specified. If this is not so, the subsequent actions specified within the rule will not be executed, since the plan is for the flow of control not to return. Even unrestrained use of GO TO in a decision table context should imply only jumping to the start of the decision tables. Any other destination would harm the logic and destroy the clarity of meaning intended through the use of decision tables in the first place. Unrestrained GO TO use, transferring control between a group of tables, can be replaced by a higher-level table that determines where to go and executes the appropriate simplified tables from the group using Call Return logic. The result is a more visible, viable control structure.

MANUAL AND AUTOMATIC TRANSLATION

If it is desirable to go further than using decision tables as design and documentation tools, it is necessary to implement the resulting decision table— to stop short of using an automatic implementation of the decision table is to lose some of its power.

A decision table can be translated manually or with a translator program or preprocessor. Translating a decision table requires determining which rule applies by evaluating input conditions. Then, with respect to the action entries of the identified rule, it requires selecting and executing the specified actions. The first task, determining the rule, might be accomplished by using a set of nested IF THEN ELSEs, which can be read vertically from a canonical decision table. The actions can be executed by using the action entries as a selection matrix and inspecting the column associated with the active rule and each action in a series of IF THEN statements.

Although it is possible to translate a table manually, if necessary, there is no certainty that it has been done correctly. Verifying this, however, is much easier than verifying a linearly coded program.

One is free to revise and experiment with a decision table if a translator or preprocessor program is available to translate it flawlessly. This is particularly helpful if the translator automatically does completeness and uniqueness checking and places the decision table in canonical form. (For additional information on translation, see Bibliography.)

CONCLUSION

There is little distinction between the design and implementation of decision tables. In addition, they can be used in both design and implementation activities of program development and modification.

Decision tables are valuable in design activities because they sharply separate control structure from required processing. Exhibiting the control structure in tabular form is a decision table documentation function; in fact, decision tables are excellent vehicles for representing systems and programs. Uniqueness and completeness properties and tests help in evaluating design quality; probes for evaluating the adequacy of testing are also facilitated. As such, decision tables are useful throughout the program life cycle.

Bibliography

Glass, Robert L. *Software Reliability Guidebook*. Englewood Cliffs NJ: Prentice-Hall Inc, 1979.

Hughes, Marion L., Shank, Richard M., and Stein, Elinor Svendson. *Decision Tables*. Wayne PA: MDI Publications, 1968.

London, Keith R. *Decision Tables*. Princeton NJ: AUERBACH Publishers, 1972.

McDaniel, Herman. *Applications of Decision Tables; a Reader*. Princeton NJ: Brandon/Systems Press, 1970.

Metzner, John R. *Decision Table Languages and Systems*. New York: Academic Press, 1977.

Montalbano, Michael. *Decision Tables*. Chicago IL: Science Research Associates, 1974.

Pollack, Solomon L., Hicks, Harry T., Jr., and Harrison, William J. *Decision Tables, Theory and Practice*. New York: Wiley-Interscience, 1971.

Sethi, I.K. and Chatterjee, B. "Conversion of Decision Tables to Efficient Sequential Testing Procedures." *Communications of the ACM*, Vol. 23, No. 5 (May 1980) 279-293.

⑥ Program Portability by Paul Oliver

INTRODUCTION

A report by the General Accounting Office [1], published in September 1977, states that the annual federal government cost of modifying computer programs to enable their correct execution on a computer different from the one for which they were originally devised is estimated at more than $450 million. Comparable industry-wide figures are not available, but it is reasonable to assume that the overall cost of software conversion is significant. Furthermore, this cost is nonproductive; conversion per se results in no direct step toward achieving corporate goals.

Research and development efforts are underway at several universities and research laboratories to determine ways of producing portable software, that is, software that is machine- and configuration-independent over a set of computer installations (see [2, 3]). At the same time, industry is reacting to the problem in a variety of ways, including softening architectural differences (e.g., there are about a half-dozen IBM 370 "derivatives") and improving emulation capabilities. Until such efforts bear practical fruit, DP organizations are faced with the prospect of expensive, disruptive conversions. The expense and disruption of a conversion, however, can be reduced, although seldom eliminated, by designing portable programs.

The motivation for portable programs, however, goes beyond these considerations. Parnas makes a convincing case for the importance of regarding programs as members of a family of programs, rather than as standalone products [2]. He regards a set of programs as a *program family* when they share so many characteristics that it pays to study these characteristics before investigating the special properties of individual programs. An example of such a family is the set of versions and releases of a manufacturer's operating system.

Parnas suggests, in effect, that programs be designed for change. The failure to do so can lead to several problems:
- Some changes will be made poorly.
- Some changes will not be made at all.
- Maintenance and equipment costs will be higher.

- Readiness will be impaired because of long completion time.
- At some point, wholesale conversions will be required.

Complete portability is probably not achievable because of irreconcilable differences in machine architectures; however, portable programs can be produced with the aid of appropriate design techniques. Whitten and de Maine give the following definitions for machine-independent, configuration-independent, and portable programs [3]:

> A source program is *machine independent* with respect to a set of computers if the program will compile, execute, and produce the same results on each computer. A machine independent program is *configuration independent* if required computer resources can be dynamically allocated during program execution, and the amount of memory available to the program does not by itself determine the amount of data that can be processed. A source program which is both machine and configuration independent over a set of computer installations is said to be *portable* with respect to these installations.

APPROACHES TO PORTABILITY

Portability can be achieved in several ways. The design approach, particularly modular programming (the organizing of a program into a number of units whose behavior is governed by a set of rules) can significantly affect portability. Another approach is parameterization, in which the machine-dependent or software-system-dependent features of a program are reduced to parameters that can be reorganized by a preprocessor and appropriately modified to render the program executable on a specific hardware/software configuration. Code constraints, with which limitations are imposed on the use of language features known to create portability problems, represent the most painful (to a programmer) way of achieving portability. Some constraints, however, are essential.

The specific approach chosen should depend in part on the goal to be achieved through portability:

- If the goal is to reduce the cost of an envisioned conversion, modularity helps. In a modular program, the nonportable features of the program (e.g., code that uses vendor-unique extensions to a standard language because of a real or imagined need to use those extensions) can be isolated into a few, identifiable modules.
- If the goal is to facilitate future design changes to the program, modularity again helps (if we can predict which design decisions are likely to change over time and thus reflect these decisions in discrete, identifiable modules).
- If the goal is to execute a given program on a variety of hardware/software systems, each different from the other, parameterization is a good approach to portability (see [4]). This approach also helps when executing programs at different sites that may or may not have different computers.

- Code constraints help in all of these situations.

These approaches are often applied in combination.

Modular Programming

There are several approaches to modular programming (see references 5, 6, 7, 8); of those that address portability, the two most common are based on processing flow within programs (the main-flow method) and the idea of levels of abstraction or decompositions (the hierarchical approach). Although the choice of approach depends on the project at hand, most installations adopt a design philosophy that is a mixture of the two. Although the two may overlap, the major difference between them is that control is retained by the top-level program module when the main-flow method is used, while it is delegated to subordinate modules when hierarchical design is used.

The Hierarchical Approach. The hierarchical approach is based on the idea of levels (e.g., the levels of control used in typical management reports). A hierarchical program to print totals at department and location levels, for instance, would be structured so that each level of the report is handled by a distinct level of the program structure.

More generally, the levels of a hierarchical program are levels of abstraction of the problem. The designer considers the problem at the highest level of abstraction and solves it in terms of functions appropriate to that level. The process is similar to mapping a geographic area by drawing maps of successively larger scales, each of the same physical size. The maps then form a hierarchy, with each level more detailed than the last.

Design cannot, however, proceed quite that neatly from top to bottom. It is always necessary to look down toward lower levels to anticipate problems and to ensure that low-level functions are already available and that their use is not precluded by poor design decisions at a higher level.

The Main-Flow Approach. The main-flow design philosophy results in the main control of the program—and possibly the file processing—being undertaken in the top-level module, the highest segment of the program structure. The size of that module can vary greatly, and larger modules may suffer from inadequate testing. These consequences are especially unfortunate because it is the size and complexity of the top-level module that tends to be related to the size and complexity of the program.

The differences in these two approaches can best be discerned through a specific example. Let us consider the design of a program to allocate memory space to other programs from a list of free spaces. The list could be in the form of a table, with each row representing a free block of space by its starting address and length. A number of additional assumptions would have to be stated in order to produce the program (e.g., no items will be added to or removed from the space list during execution of the program), but these assumptions are not pertinent at this time.

The main-flow approach (which also applies the principle of information hiding) might result in the following program structure:

- Master Control Module—controls sequencing among other modules and contains interfaces between modules. This module would also "hide" the action to be taken in case of error. Should this action change in the future, only this module would be affected.
- Free-Space List Module—consists of the functions that access information about spaces on the list and the program that adds items to the free-space list. This would be the only one that "turns" the representation of the variables that identify items on the list.
- Space Selection Module—consists of functions that select suitable space from the free-space list. The criterion used in selecting the space is known only to this module.
- Allocation Module—allocates all or part of the selected space to the requesting program. Information pertaining to the allocation of storage areas to programs (e.g., a table listing all storage areas) would be hidden in this module.

The resulting program would look something like this:

```
MASTER CONTROL
    "Initiation housekeeping"
    "Call FREE-SPACE to find candidate"
    "Call SELECT to select suitable space"
    "Call ALLOCATE to allocate space to re-
        questing program"
    "On ERROR call ERROR ACTION"
FREE-SPACE
SELECT
ALLOCATE
```

The design approach is somewhat bottom-up, in that the program components are first identified (in this case, by using the principle of information hiding) and then combined into a program.

In a top-down or hierarchical approach we might start with a single module:

```
MEMORY-ALLOCATOR
    "Get space for requesting program"
    "If no space is available take suitable error
        action"
```

At this point we would assume that there is a list of some kind identifying the space available, if any. We can refine this program by making certain decisions about the representation of the list, the order in which elements are placed in the list, and the search technique to be used. This would refine the program into:

```
MASTER CONTROL
   "Initiation housekeeping"
   "Call FREE-SPACE to find candidate"
   "Select and allocate free space to program"
   "On ERROR call ERROR ACTION"
FREE-SPACE
```

We can then decide that we will not allocate just any space but rather look for a best fit and, furthermore, that we will allocate only the space that is needed by the program and return the rest to the space pool:

```
MASTER CONTROL
   "Initiation housekeeping"
   "Call FREE-SPACE to find candidate"
   "Call SELECT. . ."
   "Call ALLOCATE. . ."
   "On ERROR call ERROR ACTION"
FREE-SPACE
SELECT
ALLOCATE
```

The resulting design is the same in both approaches; it is the design process that is different and that, were we actually to reduce the aforementioned to code, would possibly result in somewhat different code. In the main-line approach we reached as many design decisions as possible as early as possible, basing the decisions on the criterion of localizing those functions that might change in future versions of the program (e.g., the structure of the free-space list). In the hierarchical approach, we delayed design decisions; at each step in the design process we assumed as little as possible and then proceeded to refine the assumptions step by step. The motivation for refinement was, in each case, functional, with little concern given to future design changes. Even so, modularizing according to functions makes the program more maintainable and easier to modify (if such modification is required to transport the program to a system different from that for which it was designed). The fact that the modules turned out to be the same in both cases is a result of the size and simplicity of the example. This is, unfortunately, a persistent problem in attempting to illustrate software engineering concepts; the concepts are effective only with "large" programs, yet it is not feasible to use large programs for illustrative purposes.

Certain benefits can be derived from either approach. The main-flow method is easily learned by programmers familiar with conventional flowcharting techniques. The hierarchical method is more difficult to teach and apply properly.

The main-flow method tends to relate the size of the top module to the size of the program. Top-level module size in hierarchical design can remain the same regardless of program size. This makes the latter more suited to large systems, and it is frequently employed for large, real-time programs.

The main-flow technique often mirrors the processing flow within the program. This tendency, coupled with a change in the direction of program flow, can result in widespread alterations of program structure. Hierarchical design, however, tends to reflect the data structure, and any changes to this structure may necessitate program structure changes.

Like program design, construction of each module can follow a particular design philosophy. The technique used to build the modules can affect core requirements, execution time, and the amount of coding required.

Implementing Modules. Modules are generally implemented as either internal (sectional) subroutines or as independently compiled subroutines. Sectional subroutines are those that can be entered only by instructions contained in the same compilation unit. In COBOL, a section entered by a PERFORM statement is a sectional subroutine.

An independently compiled subroutine is one that can be compiled separately, placed on a library, and linked together with others by a linkage editor or its equivalent. The instruction that calls the module is contained in another object module. An independently compiled subroutine in COBOL would be executed by a CALL (module name) USING . . . statement. Although an independently compiled subroutine is more flexible than its counterpart, it can measurably increase program core requirements and execution time.

However modules are constructed, certain characteristics are desirable. It is important that each module be considered an entity, particularly if developed by different programmers. Independent specifications and documentation should be produced to allow module implementation in isolation from the rest of the program.

Each module should be capable of calling or being called by another. It is also desirable for the modules to be closed. A called module is closed if it can be CALLed from a calling module and the programmer can be certain that the program will return to the statement after the CALL in the calling module.

Several languages allow several entry points in one module. It is safer, however, to produce a structure with extra modules, each with single entry and exit points. In addition, single entry and exit points save core and facilitate maintenance.

Modules should also have a standard interface: they should be activated in the same way, pass parameters in the same way, store the contents of registers on entry and reinstate the contents on exit, and return control to the calling module.

Once again, these recommendations are not intended to reduce the changes required in transporting a program to a different machine; rather, they will make any required changes less painful.

PORTABLE FORTRAN PROCEDURES

PFORTRAN. The most systematic and comprehensive attempt at producing portable FORTRAN programs has led to the development of

PFORTRAN [3]. PFORTRAN is composed of four components:
- A set of FORTRAN statements that is a common dialect of seven FORTRAN dialects and a superset of American Standard (1966) FORTRAN [9]. The seven dialects are:

CDC 6000 FORTRAN IV
HIS 6000 FORTRAN IV
IBM 360/370 FORTRAN G
RCA SPECTRA 70 FORTRAN
XDS Sigma 5/7 FORTRAN
Sperry Univac 1108 FORTRAN V
Digital Equipment PDP-11 FORTRAN IV-PLUS

The statements included in the set are:

ASSIGN	DIMENSION	GO TO
Assignment	DO	IF
statements	END	RETURN
BLOCK	ENTRY	Statement function
DATA	EQUIVALENCE	STOP
CALL	EXTERNAL	SUBROUTINE
COMMON	FUNCTION	Type statement
CONTINUE		
DATA		

- The standard FORTRAN data type set extended to include kernels, bit strings, and virtual arrays. Kernels are variable-length data units (e.g., contiguous storage). Virtual arrays provide the means of maintaining configuration independence, since their size can exceed available memory.
- A simple, machine-independent I/O function or interface.
- A variable arithmetic package that allows the programmer to specify the numerical precision required in calculation (which allows this precision to be modified as required by the differences in word size among machines of different architectures). Unfortunately, PFORTRAN itself is not portable, since a substantial portion of it consists of assembler language support subroutines. These could, of course, be recoded.

Programming Practices. A system like PFORTRAN is not generally acceptable in a production environment. An alternative is to apply code restraints [10] that enhance a FORTRAN program's portability, such as:
- Looping (DO statements)—the following should be avoided:
  —One terminal statement for a sequence of vested loops
  —Terminating a DO-loop with an IF statement
  —Altering the looping parameters within the loop
  —Assuming a loop is always executed at least once
  —Transferring into a loop
  —Assuming the value of an index outside the loop

- Transfer of Control—the following should be avoided:
  —Recurring subroutines
  —Returning from subroutines by way of an assigned GO TO
  —Making assumptions about incorrectly computed GO TO variables
  —Variable-length arguments in subroutine calls
- Miscellaneous—the following should be avoided:
  —Testing for equality with floating-point numbers
  —Double exponentiation
  —Assumptions regarding division by zero
  —Shifting by multiplication

PORTABLE COBOL PROGRAMS

The Benchmark Preparation System (BPS). The Federal COBOL Compiler Testing Service (FCCTS), a system that produces portable COBOL programs [4], was developed in 1974. Intended for use in a benchmarking environment, the system is, in fact, generally applicable.

The Benchmark Preparation System performs conversion of application COBOL programs in the major areas affecting portability: nonstandard COBOL functions, implementor names, and data representation. A COBOL source-program translator converts native-machine COBOL programs to machine-independent COBOL (i.e., standard adhering COBOL). Those functions in the native-machine COBOL that are extensions to the ANSI language specifications (and therefore cannot be automatically converted) are flagged by the translator. Implementor names in the programs are replaced with unique names in the machine-independent source programs. These names are recognized and replaced by a preprocessor when the programs are implemented on the target machine.

Input data files associated with the programs are translated by a series of COBOL programs. These data translation programs use data conversion subroutines in the respective COBOL compilers (native or target machine) in translating the machine-dependent data to machine-independent format and vice versa. Machine-dependent data characteristics include arithmetic sign, word boundary alignment, and certain internal representations. The COBOL data translation programs are generated programmatically from the program file descriptions. File descriptions in the data translation programs are those for the native-machine file, machine-independent file, and ANSI/target file. The native-machine file description is used to read the native-machine data files and to build machine-independent data files. All data in these files will be stored in display or character mode, with the signs of numeric data stored separately. Essentially, machine-dependent data is translated to a string of characters that may then be subject to straight character-code translations for the appropriate machine.

Upon transfer of the data files to the target machine, the reverse operation occurs. The machine-independent data is read according to the file descriptions and written using the ANSI/target file descriptions. The data translation programs also provide the capability of validating the data files (e.g., numerically described fields with nonnumeric data are identified). Validation can be executed separately or performed in conjunction with creating the independent- or target-machine data files. One important feature of the BPS is that, unlike PFORTRAN, it is itself portable, since it is written in a subset of COBOL.

Programming Practices. As with FORTRAN, certain features of COBOL are known to be potential problems with regard to portability. The sources of those problems are:

- General—the program
  —Requires operator intervention in processing
  —Requires operator console input(s)
  —Has checkpoint/restart capabilities
  —Contains an interface to data base systems
  —Requires object-code patches not incorporated into the current source
  —CALLS to an assembler or other non-COBOL language subprogram
  —Uses overlays or segmentation
- IDENTIFICATION DIVISION entries
  —Entries out of order with respect to the ANS COBOL standard
- ENVIRONMENT DIVISION entries
  —FILE-CONTROL
  —I-O-CONTROL
- DATA DIVISION entries
  —FILE SECTION
  —RECORDING MODE
  —LOCK CONTAINS 0
  —USAGE IS COMP-1 short-precision floating-point data
  —COMP-2 long-precision floating-point data
  —COMP-3 internal decimal data (packed data)
  —COMP-4 binary data
- WORKING-STORAGE section
  —Logic of the program expects certain initial values when data has not been initialized
  —REDEFINES
  —OCCURS DEPENDING ON
  —Bit-level data fields (noncharacter aligned)
  —Logical switches
  —Logical masks
  —Floating-point literals
  —Floating-point fields
  —Signed zero
  —Unsigned numeric fields used in computations
  —INDEX
  —Subscripts
  —Sort description SD-names
- Linkage section
  —Linkage entries
- Report section

- —Report writer description RD-names
- Communication section
- —Communication description CD-names
- PROCEDURE DIVISION entries
- —Program logic sensitive to numeric precision
- —Program logic dependent on the collating sequence
- —Logic dependent on HIGH-VALUE or LOW-VALUE
- —Logic dependent on rounding or truncation of numeric results
- —Logical shifts or bit manipulation
- —Miscellaneous verbs including:
  ALTER
  CLOSE
  COMPUTE
  EXAMINE
  GO TO DEPENDING
  Certain MOVE statements
  OPEN
  PERFORM (but not PERFORM . . . THRU . . .)
  SEARCH
  COPY
  TRANSFORM
  WRITE
  SORT
  LABEL

Some of these practices occasionally cause portability problems because of machine differences (e.g., operation interfaces, console messages, checkpoint-restart). In most cases, however, these problems are caused by differences in the way compilers implement the COBOL language. The verb COMPUTE, for example, is defined by the COBOL standard in such a way that almost any implementation is acceptable. The only solution in cases involving verbs that are incompatible with portability is to avoid the verbs in question.

Programming standards that identify and prohibit the use of the practices and verbs previously listed encourage the production of more portable programs, but only if the standards are enforced. This enforcement must be automated to be effective (e.g., with a preprocessor that identifies standards violation and prevents compilation of an offending program).

PORTABILITY IN DATA BASE MANAGEMENT SYSTEMS

The use of data base management systems (DBMS) generally aggravates the portability problem. There has, however, been at least one successful attempt at producing a machine-independent DBMS, appropriately called MIDMS (Machine Independent Data Management System).

MIDMS was developed by the Defense Intelligence Agency and the General Electric Company in 1973. In the batch processing portion of MIDMS, 97 percent of the programming language statements are in COBOL.

MIDMS, which is composed of modules, submodules, and subroutines, has a dynamic overlay structure that permits the system to be executed using a minimal amount of main storage. The modular structure gives the system a high degree of flexibility, allows for growth, and facilitates modification. Special features of MIDMS include:

- The capability to process large variable-length records as well as the normal fixed-length record
- The capability to call subroutines and to use tables in the maintenance, retrieval, and output phases
- Special operators to perform geographic searches
- An extensive validation capability for use during the maintenance phase

In addition, using the standard MIDMS interface, the user can call COBOL, FORTRAN, or assembler language programs during maintenance, retrieval, or output processes.

MIDMS is characterized by variable-length records containing fixed, periodic, and variable sets of data. The fixed information can have only one unique value for each record (e.g., name and social security number for an employee's record in a personnel file). The system provides a second level of data elements within a record by means of the periodic set structure. Each set represents a category of information that is either empty or has one or more elements, each requiring one subset. In a personnel file where a record would apply to one employee, there might be a periodic set for the dependents category and a periodic set for the education category. The first set would contain a subset for each dependent, and the second would contain a subset for each school the employee has attended. Finally, unstructured information of unknown length (e.g., remarks) can be placed in variable sets. Thus the MIDMS concept affords space saving by compacting the data. This also leads to time saving with sequential files, since large empty areas need not be read. (If the records were of a fixed length, extensive reading would be required, since the records would have to be large enough to accommodate a maximum amount of data.) Despite its attractive features, MIDMS suffers limited use because it was not developed by a major software producer. The system does, however, provide concrete evidence that portability in a DBMS environment is possible.

CONCLUSION

Complete program portability is not practical at this stage in the DP industry's evolution. Hardware architectures are still too diverse, and there is little order in the system software arena. Until discipline and standards prevail, users must achieve a measure of portability at the expense of other program characteristics. Programmers should be encouraged to take the steps suggested in this chapter when it is economically advisable and it is anticipated that execution will be on different or diverse computer systems.

References

1. General Accounting Office Report of the Congress, FGMSD-77-34, September 15, 1977.
2. Parnas, D.L. "On the Design and Development of Program Families." *IEEE Transactions on Software Engineering*, March 1976.
3. Whitten, D.E., and de Maine, P.A.D. "A Machine and Configuration Independent FORTRAN: Portable FORTRAN (PFORTRAN)," Computer Science Department, Pennsylvania State University (1974), University Park, PA 16802.
4. Baird, G.N. and Johnson, L.A. "System for Efficient Program Portability." *Proceedings of the 1974 NCC, AFIPS, 1976.*
5. Jackson, M.A. *Principles of Program Design.* New York: Academic Press, 1975.
6. Myers, G.J. *Software Reliability.* New York: John Wiley and Sons, 1976.
7. Rohder, J. "Tackle Software with Modular Programming." *Computer Decisions,* October 1973.
8. Yourdon, E. *Techniques of Program Structure and Design.* Englewood Cliffs, NJ: Prentice-Hall, 1975.
9. "American Standard FORTRAN," American Standards Association, 1966.
10. Heiss, Joel E., et al. "Programming for Transferability." International Computer Systems, Inc. (1972), 10801 National Boulevard, Los Angeles, CA, 90064.

7 Writing Straightforward, Maintainable Programs

by James F. Gross

INTRODUCTION

The realities of a programming manager's life include keeping up with changes in hardware, system software, and user requirements while dealing constantly with upper-level budget and schedule constraints on one side and programmers' egos on the other. All of these factors must be considered in changing the view of maintenance as a crisis and a curse into the view of it as simply an expected part of the job. It must be remembered, too, that the strong influence of past maintenance experience has shaped the manager's thinking and actions, and strong positive measures are needed to counteract this generally negative opinion.

THE EFFORT AND COST OF MAINTENANCE

It would certainly make life easy—or at least easier—if a program or system could be designed, constructed, thoroughly tested, and then put into operation with never another look. Unfortunately, this ideal situation rarely happens, even with small programs; it has been said that a program that does not change is one that is probably not being used.

Why should this be the case? Before construction of the original program began, all details were carefully planned, approved, and deemed adequate—and the actual code faithfully implemented the plan. If it works, why should it require maintenance? Three situations can force modification of a program:

- There may be changes in the system itself. Normal growth of a business may require the installation of bigger and newer disks. CRTs may replace teletypes, and the program must then be changed to take advantage of the differences. Not only may the hardware change, but the system software may change as well. When a new release offers attractive capabilities, some rewriting will be essential to make use of them.
- There may be internal changes in the organization or its business. The shop becomes unionized and the payroll program must now deduct union dues, or the mortgage loan department wants to offer customers a choice of payment due dates. The customer service department may want an online inquiry capability to trace orders. Each of these situations would require some change to the DP support packages. It should be noted that

since the need to change is internal, so is the decision to change. If a modification is too costly, it may be abandoned—but, at the same time, it may send customers elsewhere.

* There may be external changes that cannot be ignored. The Internal Revenue Service reporting requirements change from time to time and must be satisfied. The proposed 9-digit ZIP code plan will require many program and file changes. Employee fringe benefit packages may change with each new contract.

Thus, no matter what the source of the need for modification, maintenance must be performed, and the costs are high. Since there are more computers, and they run faster than their predecessors, there are more programs to be maintained. Even if there were only a fixed number of systems to maintain, the expense would increase with time, as staff members—and their salaries—mature. The result is that maintenance costs make up a substantial part of the budget. Estimates indicate that 80 percent of the cost of a computer operation is software, and as much as 75 percent of that figure may be for maintenance.

The figures for programmer time are similar. A programmer who is doing maintenance on old applications is obviously not making much progress on new applications. Therefore, making programs easier to maintain will increase productivity while reducing cost. Since this fact seems to be understood and accepted, it might be wise to look more closely at why the real situation is so different from the ideal. How did DP departments get into this mess of hard-to-maintain programs? Contributing factors can be classified as the general philosophy of perfection, educational bias, tradition, laziness, and the company.

Philosophy of Perfection. This is a social viewpoint. Most consumer products are designed and constructed with the assumption that no repair for this perfect product will ever be needed. Appliances, for example, have panel lights buried inside where replacement is difficult or impossible without disassembling the whole unit. Many automobiles have notoriously complicated arrangements that cause great effort and expense when repairs are required. In some cars, even the most routine maintenance (e.g., changing spark plugs or oil filters) cannot be accomplished without elaborate equipment, considerable time, and expensive labor. In contrast, some cars are built to encourage easy maintenance and to simplify smooth operation. Dashboards that swing down to expose the switches and gauges for replacement or adjustment and owner manuals with electrical circuit diagrams reflect a different philosophy and make it quite easy for the mechanic (programmer) or buyer (user) to understand the problem and make the necessary repair. It may well be time to change the long tradition of making something without worrying about its future maintenance.

Educational Bias. Another factor to consider is the bias inherent in much programmer training. With few exceptions, from the first exposure to computer programming, the student is directed toward one-shot programs. The emphasis is on building a program from scratch, getting it running, and then going on to something else. Many systems used by beginners cater to this load-and-go mode. The concepts of libraries, copying, and linking are postponed until near the end of the school year, by which time the lesson of writing from scratch has been well learned. Even at higher levels of study where the entire class works on a system project, there is seldom preparation for going back three years later to modify it. Performance to specification is the yardstick, and often the top grades go to the students who come up with clever convoluted solutions.

Tradition. A difficulty in overcoming this educational bias is that programmers tend to do what they were taught, their instructors teach what they were taught, and so on back to the first generation of computing. In the early days of computing, programmers had reason to be concerned about the speed of a program; a few thousand cycles equalled a full second. The limited memory of perhaps only 4,000 words of core was even more confining. It demanded squeezing a great deal into and out of each instruction, relying on tricks, bit fiddling, redefining variables, and modifying actual instructions. These attitudes die hard. Furthermore, it is easy to measure and compare length of code, speed of execution, or memory required; it is far more difficult to measure ease of maintenance. It is thus apparent what managers look for and programmers work for—and why.

Laziness. It has been observed that people will avoid unpleasant jobs and what they consider excessive or unnecessary amounts of work. For most programmers, this means spending time on enjoyable coding rather than dull documenting. They can get away with this much of the time since operating instructions usually require written documentation, but little more is insisted upon. In addition, when a program has been debugged, a new assignment is frequently made immediately, with no time for documentation, which had been left for last.

The Company. The company and one's coworkers also encourage these bad habits. Consider, for example, the organization's pressures. The project status reporting form traces the stages of development: Design, Coding, Testing, and Complete. Here, it seems, debugged and finished are synonymous. To be truly finished, however, may require a week or more of organizing, writing, general cleaning up, and making the package more usable and maintainable. In some shops, the documentation for a program product is simply the most recent compilation listing. In these same shops, of course, there is always another urgent project waiting, and a programmer is strongly encouraged to get on with the new task. Time pressures and urgency preclude doing as careful and complete a job as should be done.

Fellow programmers exert pressure to continue the artful programming alluded to earlier. One seldom hears such comments as, ''Boy, that Charlie is a quiet, steady worker. His code is longer and slower than anyone else's, and it's easy to maintain.'' On the other hand, there will be much comment about Marv's new calculation that determines whether February has 29 days (it works for any year between 1700 and 2400). A whole office buzzes with admiration when Jane finds a way to replace two subroutines with one 4th-degree polynomial. It is small wonder that changing attitudes is so hard.

The Programmer as a Creative Individual

The personality of a programmer must also be considered. Most program-mers regard themselves as artists, as creative individuals with a need to personalize their work. This is really not surprising. As previously noted, most programmers have been encouraged to be inventive throughout their education.

A trainee-level programmer is doubtless given programs written by others to study, perhaps to document, and perhaps to modify slightly. Being full of new self-importance, he or she probably looks for inefficiencies, obvious construc-tions, or straightforward data formats and tries to make them all a bit more clever.

As his or her career progresses, the programmer may become a specialist in a particular area of software. Like a magician, he or she is honor-bound not to reveal any secrets. Some of the programming, of course, is nothing more than sleight of hand to keep the uninitiated from knowing what is going on by building labyrinths and using incantations known only to the wizard in order to preserve the mystery.

Less imaginative, but just as real and harmful (and quite common), is the programmer's attitude of putting something of himself or herself into a program to make it uniquely that programmer's. The programmer sees himself or herself as a painter instead of a draftsman, and the details of the code show his or her personality. It is easy to look at a listing and identify the author from the habits, preferences, and idiosyncracies that are the hallmarks of the artisan. The original author is undoubtedly quite familiar and comfortable with a certain style. Someone other than that person, unfortunately, will be assigned the subsequent modifications, and those individual touches will make things less obvious and more difficult.

This belief that programming is a creative act, not a methodical and produc-tive job, is an attitude that makes a programmer ignore the obvious solution and seek a new approach. Some of this, of course, is good. Progress depends upon a willingness to leave the well-worn paths to explore new territory. It is sense-less, however, to hack a tortuous path through underbrush if a road already exists. Later travelers will find a well-marked, well-groomed highway far easier to follow.

A BETTER PHILOSOPHY

The best way around the present state of affairs is to write programs initially with modification and maintenance in mind. Programs will change, and such change should be anticipated and accommodated. A simple parallel can be drawn with a home remodeling project. Having a shutoff valve in a plumbing line makes repairing, replacing, or rerouting the rest of the pipe easy; the best time to install that valve is during initial construction.

When a house is being framed, a gap can be left in the wall studs, where the doorway to a possible future addition would be, and a separate electrical circuit can be run to that wall for eventual connection. The cost of including these features in the original plan is very small, compared to the cost of modification after the house is finished. There is clearly some risk that the addition will never be realized, in which case the extra circuit is wasted. The benefit derived from having it available when it is needed, however, is well worth the risk.

Foresight

The decisions about what to build in and what to ignore require foresight, one of the rarest and most elusive gifts among human beings. Although there are no reliable crystal balls, historical lessons and the combined experience of several people can provide a workable substitute. One of the most important steps a programmer can take when considering future changes is to ask what possibilities exist and what their probabilities are.

To illustrate this idea, one can suppose that a new payroll file is being laid out. Foresight at the programmer's level, whether gained by bad experiences of one's own or by hearing about those of others, may suggest that it is wise to leave some extra space to allow for wages of more than $9.99, for example. But how many spare fields should be included? Is it likely that the company will establish a credit union or that it will allow employees to purchase stock through payroll deductions? Answering questions such as these requires a knowledge of long-range fiscal policy. Since the programmer does not have such information, he or she must consult someone who does.

In addition to considering the various options, it is important to let others know what has been done. Like a blueprint notation about the future doorway, the possibilities for change must be included in the original documentation. There is only a minor difference in the effort involved in specifying a field adjacent to the STATE part of a customer's address as FILLER and specifying it as ZIP-GROWTH. The difference means very little additional work at the time, and the field might never be needed. Making the intention clear, however, will also make it clear to those who follow. It may also protect the field from the programming whiz who sees this as an opportunity to eliminate a 4-column filler from every record.

A Team Effort

The next part of the new philosophy may be harder for programmers to accept since it may signal the end of the golden age when the programmer was king. The new view is that a program is a job to be done and a task to be accomplished, instead of a monumental work of art for the glorification of the individual who does it. There are to be no more wizards, just steady, reliable coders: team members. There is to be good sound code that is easy to understand and maintain; there are to be portable programs. The workers are master craftsmen, not artists. This view should not be construed as deprecating the programmers' craft; their skills will still be admired and rewarded, but in different ways.

Programmers may find this concept hard to accept because they lose much immediate praise and glory. If they have come to depend upon the approval and admiration of their peers, it will take a long time to adjust to the loss. They will find in time, however, that there is less stress in the job, for they no longer have to worry about finding the cleverest way. If the job is a modification, for example, it will be clearer where and how to make the changes, and the programmers will simply do them. Their satisfaction will then come from doing the job correctly and quickly, with a resulting overall improvement. As users become more sympathetic to the need for planning ahead, they will offer more suggestions regarding future situations.

A group that works more closely together provides additional rewards. The programmer has questions, and the supervisor either has answers or can get them. The programmer has suggestions about how to build for future changes; the supervisor considers and discusses those suggestions. Since the programs— the actual code—will be clearer, the manager will be able, when necessary, to look at particulars without needing a great deal of time to study them. Keeping closer track of the progress of a job allows the manager to make directions more specific, relieving the programmer of the need to make some of the stress-producing decisions.

Accurate Reports and Schedules. Keeping in closer touch will also help the manager plan ahead. If things are going smoothly (and possibly faster than expected), additional projects can be planned. If there is a snag or if some questions are still awaiting answers from upper management, there is more advance warning that the job will be late. Even long deadline slips can be accommodated with enough advance warning. The worst problems arise when everything is assumed to be proceeding nicely and, at the last minute, one component knocks the schedule off course. A bank, for example, is planning to institute a new service on June 1. The ads have been run, brochures printed and distributed, dignitaries invited (months ahead) to the ribbon cutting, and then, a few days before instituting the service, a programmer reveals that it is not quite finished. Hurrying to meet the deadline creates even more problems, of course; accurate progress reports would have warned of the slippage and saved the bank embarrassment.

There are other long-range benefits to be gained from sensible program design. Money may be saved by modifying instead of rewriting. Under the old rules, so much time was spent figuring out how a program worked in the first place and then figuring out how to change it, that modifications were often abandoned in favor of building a new system. The reputation of the DP department within the company may improve when things go haywire less frequently, and awkward procedures and formats can be adjusted more easily.

BENEFITS OF STANDARDS

Working within standards promotes clarity and maintainability in programs. The use of standards protects against individualism, which is crucial in any system where the originator of a task will probably not be its modifier.

Levels of Standards

What standards are there in programming? Generally, there are two levels (which are not in conflict): those of the organization and those of the language.

Organizational Standards. Just as telephone companies have stated rules about what red wire is used for, so most programming groups adhere to their own internal standards. These must be in written form, and they must be reviewed periodically. If they are not, the programmers might stray from them and train new staff members in their own versions of the standards, very quickly making the standards worthless. Although it may be assumed that computer people are alert to the dangers of multiple standards (based on their experience with hardware/software, communications protocols, and other notorious incompatibilities), this is not the case.

The kinds of standards the organization sets up usually cover such things as program naming or numbering conventions, the use of copy libraries, whether or not to use middle initials, and what color the punched cards should be. The standards should go far beyond these superficial specifications, however, and include some guiding principles to help the programmer make consistent decisions. If two data entries seem inconsistent, which should take precedence? Should both be rejected? Should all programs include some optional user instruction displays? Which is generally more critical, space or time? Understanding organizational standards in these areas will eliminate some of the recurring questions of design and help guide the programmer to a design that is consistent with others.

Language Standards. The language also has standards, usually those of the American National Standards Institute (ANSI). Nearly all of the vendor-supplied compilers recognize and work with the standard syntax, and nearly all offer their own extensions to the standard. This is not surprising, since an extension gives the vendor a slight competitive edge, allowing more effective use of certain hardware features. For the most part, the extensions are good, and it is tempting to use them.

This temptation, unfortunately, must be avoided in order to write maintainable software. As should be obvious, real difficulties will arise when new and different-vendor hardware comes along. To allow a change of vendors without a concomitant need to retool the entire software library, it would be wise to stick with the standards. This will also permit more continuity between programmers. In situations where the use of added features is allowed, one person may get into the habit of using a given construction, while another person never uses it. That means unfamiliarity with the program and the need to learn new methods, both of which increase the time required to do a modification.

TECHNIQUES

There are a variety of ways to make programs better and easier to maintain. The techniques described in the following paragraphs are based on experience and research. Some may be familiar; all will be helpful.

Modular Design. The highest-level technique, with the greatest effect over the life of a software package, is using the top-down approach and a modular design. For all but the simplest programs, this technique clarifies the function of each segment and the interrelationships between segments. Problems are usually isolated in an individual module, and the maintenance effort can be concentrated in that part. There may be temptations to bend this rule and combine similar modules or put two functions into one unit. Although there might be a situation where program length is critical or some other compelling reason exists to do this, every step taken away from modularity is a step toward complicated maintenance.

Most telephone equipment, for example, is now modular: this makes repair or modification more efficient. If the cord is damaged, any customer can simply unclip it and install a new one. One style of phone can be exchanged for another, without tools or knowledge of the circuitry. The analogy is clear: it should be possible for any programmer to modify or replace a section of a system as easily as that.

Computers themselves are modular. Although hardware alterations are uncommon, parts can fail. Replacement of components that have failed is a matter of removing a board or a chip and plugging in a new one. When programs are modular, a single functional piece that is no longer doing the job (perhaps because the definition of the job has changed slightly) can be pulled out entirely and a new piece put in. (As with its hardware counterpart, this new software module should be tested before installation.)

Program modules should be as specific in their functions as possible. For given inputs, they produce certain outputs, with (ideally) no side effects. If a program has options, it is better to call or not call a particular procedure than to call one that sometimes does one thing and sometimes another.

Using Variables. Second in importance to the structured approach is building to accommodate the needs and possibilities of the future. In carpentry, for example, later changes are much easier if screws are used instead of nails and glue. If the project is a bookcase, perhaps movable shelf brackets can be installed. The result is every bit as good as one with fixed shelves, the cost is comparable, and changes can be made without calling in the original carpenter. This can be accomplished in programs primarily by using variables instead of constants. As another example, when dealing with sales tax computations, SALES-TAX-RATE should be used rather than 0.04 or 0.06. When the legislature raises the tax rate, resetting this variable will affect all of the separate computations that use it, eliminating any danger of changing all but one. If the programming language allows it, this use of variables can also apply to lists and tables, letting them grow or shrink as needed.

The concept is certainly not new; many special-purpose systems for statistics and engineering problems allow users to specify formats and select options by means of control cards. In production programs, although it is rare to require or to allow that degree of freedom, it can be considered. If there is some convenient way to input the parameters for the situation, the program can be built to behave differently, without recompiling and linking. If the options are explained sufficiently, the user can tailor the content or form of his or her results, without bothering the programming staff, just as one can replace a telephone cord or rearrange the bookshelves.

Obviously, determining what should be fixed and what should be variable means inquiring and speculating about future possibilities. Like the house addition that never gets built, some options in a program may never be activated; however, it is still less costly to put them in originally than to rewrite to accommodate the changes later.

There is a danger, of course, of carrying flexibility too far. The real and practical world must be kept in mind. Specific, rather than general, approaches should be used wherever the former are adequate. It is foolish to build a program whose output will adjust itself to any paper width from 2 to 20 inches: the chances of that range being necessary are extremely small. Furthermore, if as much time and energy are spent on tricks for easy maintenance as were previously spent on tricks for fast execution or short code, there is obviously no overall gain. The point is to abandon the idea of tricks entirely, and the goal is increased productivity at present and in the future. Looking ahead and using these techniques in the original code will not increase the time needed to get it in working condition, but may decrease it instead. Debugging, after all, is just early maintenance: the program is modified to behave differently (i.e., correctly).

Documentation. Documenting the decision process can be a great help when modifications are called for. Why a particular structure or technique was chosen (in addition to what it is) should be recorded for later viewers. Some choices may be arbitrary and not based on careful analysis; where such analysis has been done, however, the need to redo it can be avoided by passing on the original considerations and insights.

How many times has one programmer taken a listing to the original author to ask why it was done in this way? Then the author must try to remember something that may have been done long before. If there is any documentation (perhaps comments in the code itself) supporting the choice, the question need not be asked. The time required for such explanations is usually not figured into the schedule in any case, nor is it included in progress report forms; from an official point of view, it is wasted time. Even if the author has moved to another job, retired, or died, the successor can still understand the reasons. Lacking such records, some well-meaning but still-ignorant maintenance programmer may switch to an alternative that had been tried and abandoned.

Documenting should be done as the code is written, for several reasons. First, there is the motivation factor: a programmer who is in the midst of the original code is intensely interested in it, knows what it is about, and knows why he or she is doing things in certain ways. Second, there is the time factor: if comments are part of the original coding forms, the cards are already where they belong, which is obviously faster than hand-inserting them later or editing them into a file copy. Third, there is the schedule problem: as noted earlier, when at last a program runs, there is pressure to consider it completed and go on to something else. If the work of documenting is done along the way, then when the program is finished, it is really finished.

Managers must also consider what could be done if the programmer were to leave tomorrow. That brings a sharp focus to the consequences of not annotating work. Some of the best organizing and documenting occurs when a conscientious programmer knows that he or she is leaving. There is a need to tidy up, to organize, and to make it comfortable for the newcomer. This results in a smooth transition but takes a week or two of redoing rough work, indexing, filing, and discarding. Time will be saved if the manager insists that this kind of effort be a part of the ongoing development.

An article in a local paper recently described the chaotic state of that city's DP system. The system was in danger of collapsing because of a succession of programmers who modified without documenting and then moved out. The result was ridiculous performance, no understanding about what was happening, and the hiring of an outside firm on a quarter-million-dollar contract to straighten out the mess.

Reasonable Shorthand. In addition to the liberal use of remarks within the code, one of the simplest and most effective aids to understanding is the use of meaningful names for variables, procedures, and files. FORTRAN's restriction to six characters still allows the use of reasonable shorthand. An example of the problems caused by ignoring the possible effect of names comes from life. The value of PI in a program was given as 6.2832. Apparently the young programmer, in his first encounter with spherical trigonometry, started out with the value of pi as 3.1416 and then discovered that he needed to use two pi. The easiest fix was to redefine the variable as shown. The program worked well, since computers do not care what names are used. Other programmers, however, certainly do care. When the time came to correct another problem (the original writer had, of course, left for another job), the 3.1416 value was taken for granted, and the variable PI was used in some of the changes. When the changes blew up, a considerable amount of detective work was required to reveal the culprit.

A less serious example cropped up in a COBOL program with a procedure named WRTHDING. On initial reading and for some time after, this was thought to mean WORTH DOING—a strange label indeed. Closer inspection of the code within the procedure made it clear that the name was a compressed form of WRITE HEADING, which should have been said initially. The reason it was not may have been laziness and or an attempt to perpetuate the mystique. Programmers must be reminded not to do this; the goal should and must be clarity.

Ordered Arrangement. Another helpful habit is to arrange both variable and procedure names in order so that the future reader does not have to look through listings for a needle in a haystack of code. Unless core storage is extremely precious and word boundaries must be considered, unrelated variables can be assigned to any locations. They might be arranged in alphabetical order so that rather than looking through the entire data division for METER-READING-START, only the M section is viewed.

A similar benefit results from keeping procedure names or statement numbers in general low-to-high sequence. (With alphanumeric labels, this means keeping part of the name, perhaps a prefix or suffix, as a numeric.) When a transfer of control occurs, the value of the destination itself gives an indication of where (within the whole program) it can be found. PAGE-HEADING-PRINT-1000, for example, would be somewhere after FORM-AVERAGE-COST-600. Some programmers' or organization standards reserve certain blocks of numbers for particular functions. All FORMATs may be grouped at the end with numbers in the 9000s, or all procedures ending with 500s may be I/O routines. Whatever the convention, consistency and documentation make follow-up modifications easier.

Interactions. Interactions among the parts must be considered when designing and implementing in a modular fashion. As an illustration, there is a module for printing some summary information, and there is a variable keeping concurrent count of the number of lines on the page. Ideally, the printing module should do only the printing; the next higher level segment that invoked the printing would advance the line counter. This has the desirable property of restricting what the printing module does. Unfortunately, it also implies that a change within the printing module shortening or lengthening the output causes a separate change to be made to the calling module. This side effect must be dealt with and should be noted in the original documentation. Such interactions can be minimized by using global variables or explicit parameters, which does, however, dilute the strength of modularity.

Classifications. A series of simple decisions should be used to make classifications. Frequently, however, many decisions and branches are lined up, one after another. There is usually an implicit none-of-the-above category that drops through all the decisions to the statement following the series of tests. This is clearly the intention in a simple two-way choice. In a longer list, however, the "other" category should be made explicit so that the default below it becomes an error indicator. This provides one small measure of protection against unexpected values and makes it easy to insert one more valid condition test at a later time.

CONCLUSION

These recommendations for design and coding reflect the general philosophy of planning for change. Every minute spent concentrating on clarity and flexibility during initial construction will be saved many times in maintenance time. Although programs may be slightly longer or slower, machinery is not the costly component today—people are. At least as important as the monetary rewards are the personal rewards. Managers will be more content because schedules and budgets are more realistic and reliable. Supervisors will be happier because users are more satisfied and there is closer contact with the staff. Programmers, too, will be more satisfied because they are doing a better job, with less pressure and far less frustration. It should be noted that these personal rewards translate into increased productivity and ultimately into dollars.

⑧ Programming Style in COBOL

by George N. Baird

INTRODUCTION

The vast increase in the ratio of computing power to cost during the past decade has not been accompanied by a similar rise in the ratio of programming productivity to cost. Execution efficiency was extremely important when computers had small memories, and the cost of hardware performance was high. The cost of the time spent producing execution-time-efficient programs today, however, may never be recovered, and the programs may cause additional maintenance costs—the efficiency techniques might not be understood by the next programmer.

Current trends in software development are toward the enhancement of existing code and less production of new source code. The higher the quality of the source code, the lower the cost of maintaining or enhancing the programs.

Programming style dictates the degree of maintainability. At one time, programmers were frequently treated like temperamental artists and given free rein in the methodologies they used to develop programs. Any attempt to standardize programming styles or techniques was considered an attempt to stifle creativity.

Many new programmers still believe that there is virtue in producing programs using a minimum of source statements. (They also frequently use ADD, SUBTRACT, and MOVE CORRESPONDING statements in trying to reduce the number of statements in the procedure division.) This generally leads to programs that are very difficult to maintain.

As programmers' salaries continue to rise, so do maintenance costs (which consume most of the time spent on software). It is now obvious that adopting and enforcing programming standards can help to keep the costs of software manageable. This chapter provides guidelines for producing easily maintained and enhanced source programs.

DESIGN CONSIDERATIONS

Several criteria determine the level of maintainability of a program. The structural design (or lack of it) is probably the most important factor in determining the level of difficulty. A program should be put together in a logical fashion, with each discrete function or set of related functions isolated in a code segment or module. There should be no wild branches (GO TOs) out of or into a code segment. A top-down structured design approach with a code segment to handle each function will result in a highly structured program. (See Procedure Division section of this chapter for further definition and discussion of code segments.)

Readability, the second most important factor in determining the level of maintainability, concerns the ease with which a programmer can understand the design and processing logic of a source program. User-defined names should be as descriptive as possible. IPT-FILE-1, for example, would be better stated as TRANSACTION-INPUT-FILE; L-CTR is more readable as REPORT-LINE-COUNTER.

While such short names as SSN for social security number might be readily understood, programmers should not hesitate to use long descriptive names. User-defined names in COBOL can be up to 30 characters in length, and hyphens should be used to separate the words (e.g., EMPLOYEE-NUMBER, not EMPLOYEENUMBER).

When creating data and procedure names, programmers should make sure these names cannot be confused with others. It would be easy, for example, to confuse SWTCH-1 and SWITCH 1. Only one statement, clause, or phrase per line should be coded, except for data description entries (discussed later). A top-down design with well-defined names results in a program that is more easily read than one that uses some of the traditional nonstructured techniques.

General Guidelines

Code Formatting. Coding conventions must be stringent. All programs in a given installation should be stylized, that is, coded using these conventions so that they appear to have been produced by the same person. Maintenance programmers will thus not have to deal with varying programming styles.

The current interactive source-program development environment in which programmers enter and modify their own programs makes it easier for them not to follow standard coding conventions. In such circumstances, commercially available utility packages that produce neatly formatted source programs can be used. This approach may represent a cost-effective alternative to forcing programmers to adhere to coding conventions when producing and modifying source programs. (Subsequent sections of this chapter provide coding and formatting guidelines for each of the four divisions of a COBOL program.)

Comments. All source programs should contain comments that describe the function of each module or code segment. Descriptive comments should be used when the code is not self-explanatory.

It must be remembered that comments, in order to be useful, must be accurate. Comments addressing modified code that are not updated to reflect the change in the source code can detract from the maintainability of the program. No comments would be better than those that are inaccurate or misleading.

Punctuation

The period is the only punctuation required in COBOL. It terminates sentences in the procedure division, data and file description entries in the Data Division. Although commas and semicolons can be used to highlight the end of phrases, clauses, or statements, their use can detract from the readability of a program and can hide potential logic errors. Some high-speed printers produce almost indistinguishable commas and periods, especially if the ribbon is not fresh. Because this can confuse the logic in the procedure division (particularly in IF and other conditional statements), the use of commas and semicolons should be avoided completely.

IDENTIFICATION DIVISION

The identification division names the source program and author. It is also an ideal place to include program comments describing function, general terms, and the file and parameters necessary for execution. When maintenance or enhancement is performed on the program, the name of the maintainer should be recorded as well as the date and the goal of the maintenance.

ENVIRONMENT DIVISION

The environment division tailors the source program to a specific hardware configuration and is thus defined by the implementor. In the following example, the SELECT statement uses the one-phrase-per-line guideline, making it easy to read the code and understand the file's attributes quickly.

```
8    12
     FILE-CONTROL
     SELECT MASTER-FILE ASSIGN TO IMPLEMENTOR-NAME-1
          ORGANIZATION IS INDEXED
          RECORD KEY IS ACCOUNT-NUMBER
          ALTERNATE RECORD KEY IS SOCIAL-SECURITY-NUMBER
          ACCESS MODE IS DYNAMIC.
     SELECT . . .
```

DATA DIVISION

File Descriptions

File description entries (e.g., FD, SD) should be coded one clause per source line. FD should be coded:

```
8    12
FD   TRANSACTION-INPUT-FILE
     LABEL RECORDS ARE STANDARD
     BLOCK CONTAINS 10 RECORDS
     RECORD CONTAINS 160 CHARACTERS
     DATA RECORD IS TRANSACTION-RECORD.
     . . .
```

Saving two source lines in the following example in no way makes up for its lack of readability.

```
8     12
FD    TRANSACTION-INPUT-FILE LABEL RECORDS STANDARD
      BLOCK CONTAINS 10 RECORDS RECORD CONTAINS 160
      CHARACTERS DATA RECORD IS TRANSACTION-RECORD.
      . . .
```

Record Descriptions

The record description entries for a file should (when possible) completely define the record(s) contained in that file. Disguising a record's true description by reading or writing it with one description and operating on it in the working storage section under another should not be permitted.

Data Descriptions

Only for data description entries can the one-clause-per-source-line guideline be relaxed because many of these entries have only a PICTURE or a PICTURE and VALUE clause. In this case, coding the entire entry on a single line actually increases its readability. The PICTURE clause should begin in a specific column (36 or 40) and be aligned throughout the data division; PIC should be used instead of PICTURE. The VALUE clause could start in column 52. If a literal of 11 characters or less is used in a VALUE clause, it should be coded on the same line. If it is longer, it should begin on the next source line. Any other clauses used in describing the data item should appear on successive lines, indented to column 36 or 40 under the PICTURE clause.

```
8     12                          40                52
01    DATA-ITEM GROUP.
      03  ALPHA-ITEM              PIC X(15)         VALUE SPACE.
      03  NUMBER-ITEM             PIC S9(6)         VALUE ZERO
                                  USAGE COMP        SYNC RIGHT.
      03  NAME-FIELD
          05  LAST-NAME           PIC X(12)         VALUE SPACE
          05  FIRST-NAME          PIC X(12)         VALUE SPACE
          05  MIDDLE-INITIAL      PIC X             VALUE SPACE.
      03  BIG LITERAL             PIC X(60)         VALUE
      "THIS IS A BIG LITERAL-LONGER THAN 11 CHARACTERS".
```

Subordinate entries should be indented four character positions to clearly show the hierarchy of the data descriptions.

```
      128                         40
01    RECORD-1                    VALUE SPACE
      03  ADDRESS-LINE.
          05  STREET              PIC X(15).
          05  TOWN-STATE-ZIP.
              07  TOWN-STATE.
                  09  TOWN        PIC X(15).
                  09  STATE       PIC X(2).
              07  ZIP             PIC X(5).
      02  NAME
      . . .
```

Several current philosophies on subordinate-level numbers suggest increments of 2, 5, or 10; others suggest 1:

```
01                          01
    05                          02
        10                          03
            15                          04
```

The number actually used makes no difference; however, the organization's guidelines should require a consistent method of incrementing the numbers.

Tables/Arrays

Tables in COBOL are defined by using the OCCURS clause in the data description entry of an item that is to be repeated within the table/array. When defining a table/array, a numeric data item should also be defined and initialized to a value that equals the occurrences of the table. The data item can then be referenced in the procedure division, in lieu of a numeric literal, when a value must be checked against the size of the table. This facilitates changing the table size without requiring a search through the procedure division to change numeric literals to reflect the new table length. With this technique, all references to table size are changed automatically; this eliminates the possibility of a missed reference causing the program to work incorrectly.

```
01    TABLE-DEFINITIONS.
      03 TABLE-1-LENGTH          PIC 9(3) VALUE 500.
      03 TABLE-1
         05 TABLE-1-ENTRY        PIC X(20)
                                 OCCURS 500 TIMES
                                 INDEXED BY INDEX-1.

IF TABLE-1-ENTRY (INDEX-1) EQUAL TO
   PERFORM . . .
IF INDEX-1 EQUAL TABLE-1-LENGTH
   GO 1 TO TABLE-PROCESS-EXIT.
SET INDEX-1 UP BY 1.
```

TABLE-1-LENGTH represents the length of TABLE-1 and can be used in the procedure division to determine whether subscripts or indexes are within the proper range.

PROCEDURE DIVISION

Code Segments or Modules

A code segment or module is a related set of procedures that are necessary to perform a single function. A section with one or more paragraphs or a series of paragraphs with a common exit point can constitute a code segment or module. A single entry point at the beginning and a single exit point at the end of the code segment are necessary. There should be no entry into a code segment at other than the entry point, and control should not leave a code segment except at the exit point. A section name is referenced in a PERFORM statement. A series of paragraphs is referenced in a PERFORM statement using the THRU phrase, naming the beginning and exit point paragraphs:

Section

```
PERFORM PROCESS-PARAMETERS
   . . .

PROCES-PARAMETERS SECTION
PROC-PARAM-001
   . . .

PROCESS-PARAMETERS-EXIT
   EXIT.
NEXT SECTION.
   . . .
```

Paragraph

```
PERFORM PROCESS-PARAMETERS THRU PROCESS-PARAMETERS-EXIT.
   . . .

PROCESS-PARAMETERS.
   . . .

PROCESS-PARAMETERS-EXIT.
   EXIT.
   . . .
```

The following procedure division fragment of a COBOL program should be considered:

```
8       12
PROCEDURE DIVISION.
MAIN-SEGMENT SECTION.
MAIN-001.
        PERFORM PROGRAM-INITIALIZATION.
        PERFORM OPEN-FILE-1-INPUT.
        PERFORM OPEN-FILE-2-OUTPUT.
*--PROCESS PARAMETERS
*--
        PERFORM OPEN-PARAMETER-FILE.
        PERFORM PROCESS-PARAMETERS
            UNTIL END-OF-PARAMETERS.
        PERFORM CLOSE-PARAMETER-FILE.
*--
*-- PROCESS FILE-
*--
        PERFORM COPY-INPUT-FILE
            UNTIL END-OF-FILE-1.
        PERFORM CLOSE-FILE-1.
        PERFORM CLOSE-FILE-2.
*--
*-- PROCESS FILE COMPARE
*--
        PERFORM OPEN-FILE-1-INPUT.
        PERFORM OPEN-FILE-2-INPUT.
        PERFORM COMPARE-FILES
            UNTIL (END-OF-FILE-1
            AND END-OF-FILE-2).
        PERFORM CLOSE-FILE-1.
        PERFORM CLOSE-FILE-2.

        STOP RUN.
*-- All referenced code segments follow.
```

```
PROCESS-PARAMETERS SECTION.
  . . .
COPY-INPUT-FILE SECTION.
  . . .
COMPARE-FILES SECTION.
  . . .
OPEN-FILE-1-INPUT SECTION.
  . . .
OPEN-FILE-2-INPUT SECTION.
  . . .
CLOSE-FILE-1 SECTION.
  . . .
CLOSE-FILE-2 SECTION.
  . . .
READ-FILE-1 SECTION.
  . . .
READ-FILE-2 SECTION.
  . . .
WRITE-FILE-2 SECTION.
  . . .
PROGRAM-INITIALIZATION SECTION.
  . . .
```

As indicated in this source code, the main segment provides a table of contents for the program:

- Initialization takes place.
- Files are opened and input parameters processed.
- One file is copied to another.
- Files are closed and reopened for the next operation.
- The two files are compared.
- The files are closed.
- Processing is terminated.

Code that would, by its clutter, affect the readability of the main module (e.g., initialization code and the I/O statements for each file) are coded as modules and referenced through a PERFORM statement. These modules are placed toward the end of the procedure division since they are easily debugged, contain simple (if any) logic, and rarely need to be seen during maintenance or enhancement.

A further refinement of the code in the main segment might be to include the references to opening and closing the files in their respective processing modules:

```
PROCEDURE DIVISION.
MAIN-SEGMENT SECTION
MAIN-001.
    PERFORM PROGRAM-INITIALIZATION.
    PERFORM PROCESS-PARAMETERS
        UNTIL END-OF-PARAMETERS.
    PERFORM COPY-INPUT-FILE
        UNTIL END-OF-FILE-1.
    PERFORM COMPARE-FILES
        UNTIL END-OF-FILE-1
            AND END-OF-FILE-2.
    STOP RUN.
```

PROCESS-PARAMETERS SECTION
. . .

Note the added clarity and simplification of the main segment after the removal of references to file opening and closing modules.

A code segment should begin at the top of a page in the compilation listing using ''/'' in column 7 of the source line prior to the beginning paragraph or section. The segment should not be larger than one page of code (e.g., 50 to 55 lines). This relieves programmers of the need to skim several pages of listings in order to read a single code segment or module.

The PERFORM statement is the only permissible way to execute code segments. The UNTIL phrase of the PERFORM statement is used to control the iteration, or looping, of code segments that must be executed until a specific condition is satisfied. A variable to be incremented during execution of a code segment is controlled by the VARYING phrase of the PERFORM statement.

The GO TO

Much has been written about GO TO and about programming that does not use it. COBOL was designed before GO TO fell from favor; thus, the statement is used. It should be limited, however, because it is very easy to GO TO the wrong place and produce a hard-to-find logic error. Moreover, a clearly structured program is difficult to produce unless the use of GO TO is restricted.

As indicated in these guidelines, the PERFORM statement is a far better tool for executing a code segment and ensuring proper return of control. PERFORM controls looping or iteration in the same manner. When GO TO is used, it should always reference a procedure name in the same code segment that is forward of the statement (a backward reference would constitute looping or iteration).

I/O Statements

Each I/O statement for a file should be isolated in a code segment and referenced through a PERFORM statement. Only one I/O statement of each type should exist for any file (e.g., READ, WRITE, OPEN); this eases required maintenance or enhancement. A condition, name, or data item can provide status information about an I/O statement to the code segment referencing it:

```
01    EOF-CONDITION-FILE-1 PIC X(3) VALUE SPACE
        88 END-OF-FILE-1 VALUE "YES".
        . . .

      PERFORM READ-FILE-1
      IF END-OF-FILE-1
        . . .

READ-FILE-1 SECTION.
R-FILE-1-001.
        IF END-OF-FILE-1
            GO TO R-FILE-1-EXIT.
```

```
          READ FILE-1 AT END
              MOVE "YES" TO EOF-CONDITION-FILE-1.
      R-FILE-1-Exit.
          EXIT.
```

IF Statements and Nested IF Statements

The code should be indented to reflect the hierarchy of control when the IF statement is used:

```
IF AGE LESS THAN 21
      PERFORM PROCESS-MINOR
ELSE
      PERFORM PROCESS-ADULT.
ADD . . .
```

The ELSE phrase (if present) should be aligned under the IF statement. The indentation clearly delineates which code is subordinate to the IF statement (executed if the condition is true) and to the ELSE phrase (executed if the condition is false).

IF statements should not be nested more than three deep. Further nesting results in logic that is difficult to understand. The following represents an IF statement nested three deep:

```
IF condition-1
      statement-1
      IF condition-2
          statement-2
          IF condition-3
              statement-3
          ELSE
              statement-4
      ELSE
          IF condition-4
              statement-4
ELSE statement-7
      IF condition-5
          statement-8
          IF condition-6
              statement-9
          ELSE
              statement-10
      ELSE statement-11
          IF condition-7
              statement-12
          ELSE
              statement-13.
```

Other Conditional Statements

Several statements (other than IF) contain conditionally executed source code. This code should be indented to identify it as well as its range. Unlike the IF statement, the ELSE clause is not associated with conditional statements, which include the following:

- ON SIZE ERROR clause of the arithmetic statements

- AT END/INVALID KEY clauses of the I/O statements
- WHEN and AT END clauses of the SEARCH statement
- ON OVERFLOW clause of the CALL statement
- NO DATA clause of the RECEIVE statement

General Coding Practice for the Procedure Division

All of the previous examples of procedure division source code have followed the one-statement/clause-per-source-line guideline. Statements that do not include or use subordinate clauses should be coded on a single source line.

```
8     12
      ADD THIS-MONTH-HOURS TO YTD-HOURS.
      MOVE ACCOUNT-NAME TO REPORT-NAME.
```

Statements with subordinate clauses should follow the same guidelines. The ADD statement can have an ON SIZE ERROR clause, which is executed when the result of the addition is too large to be stored in the receiving operand.

```
8     12
      ADD THIS-MONTH-HOURS- TO YTD-HOURS
          ON SIZE ERROR
              PERFORM HOURS-ERROR-ROUTINE.
```

The ON SIZE ERROR clause is on the line following the ADD statement; this clause is indented to show that it is part of the ADD statement. The conditionally executed source code is on the next source line; it is indented further to show that it is the conditionally executed source code associated with the ON SIZE ERROR clause.

The SEARCH statement that follows is a good example of the use of the source-code iteration technique. The WHEN clause is executed if the desired entry is found; AT END is executed if it is not found.

```
8     12
01    TABLE-GROUP-2.
      03  TABLE-2 OCCURS 100 TIMES
          ASCENDING KEY IS SOCIAL-SECURITY-NUMBER
          INDEXED BY INDEX-2.
      04  TABLE-ENTRY.
          05  DISCOUNT-RATE                                PIC V99.
          · · ·
      SEARCH ALL TABLE-2
          WHEN DISCOUNT-RATE EQUALS TRANSACTION-DISCOUNT-RATE
              PERFORM PROCESS-TRANSACTION
          AT END
              PERFORM DISCOUNT-RATE-ERROR.
```

CONCLUSION

The programming and coding techniques discussed in this chapter are intended to enable programmers to produce COBOL source code that is easy to read and understand. It should be noted that these techniques are not absolutes and should be modified to meet the particular needs of a programming shop. The purpose of using a standardized methodology is to produce stylized, consistent programs.

Consistency makes programs easier to test and debug. This, in turn, leads to a reduction in the time and cost of maintenance because the staff responsible for this function will be familiar with the style used in producing the programs.

The many software tools that can help in enforcing programming standards should be fully exploited. In a labor-intensive industry such as one that produces computer software, it is essential to do everything possible to reduce labor and control the spiraling cost of software.

Bibliography

Chmura, Louis J. "COBOL with Style—Programming Proverbs." Rochelle Park NJ: Hayden Book Co Inc, 1976.

Cohn, Lawrence S. "Effective Use of ANS COBOL Computer Programming Language." New York NY: Wiley-Interscience, 1975.

⑨ The Skeleton Program Approach to Standard Implementation

by David Schechter

INTRODUCTION

The skeleton program concept presupposes the availability of a source-program library—a direct-access facility in which source code can be stored and from which code can be copied into any program. Source libraries generally are supported by utility programs that enable particular members to be reproduced and, at the same time, assigned new names.

BUILDING THE SKELETON PROGRAM

There are seven stages in the development and customization of the skeleton program and its descendants.

First Stage. Encoding file and record descriptions used in several programs before specifying the programs that will deploy these resources is a fairly common procedure. The encoded descriptions are cataloged in the source library (see Figure 9-1).

The utility program that catalogs entries in the source library is generally insensitive to the syntax of the programming language in which the entries have been coded. A COBOL file description, for example, will not be syntax-checked by the source-library utility program.

The skeleton program began as a vehicle to verify the syntactic correctness of each copyable entry in the source library. In a COBOL environment, the first item of business is to identify the source computer and object computer. Using the IBM utility IEBUPDTE as the source librarian, this would be accomplished by running the following job step:

```
/ / UPDATE     EXEC   PGM=IEBUPDTE
/ / SYSPRINT   DD     SYSOUT=A
/ / SYSUT1     DD     DISP=SHR, DSN=COPYLIB
/ / SYSUT2     DD     DISP=SHR, DSN=COPYLIB
/ / SYSIN      DD     *
. / ADD NAME=SRCCOM
```

```
        *-------
        *SOURCE-COMPUTER. COPY SRCCOM.
        *-------
            IBM-370 WITH DEBUGGING MODE.
        *
    . / ADD NAME=OBJCOM
        *-------
        *OBJECT-COMPUTER. COPY OBJCOM.
        *-------
            IBM-370.
    . / ENDUP
```

Now, in order to prove that the code just added to the source statement library is valid COBOL code, the nucleus of a COBOL program skeleton must exercise the COPY statements and thereby fetch previously cataloged library members.

The nucleus of the COBOL program skeleton is as follows:

```
        IDENTIFICATION DIVISION.
        PROGRAM-ID.                    SKELETON-PROGRAM.
        ENVIRONMENT DIVISION.
        CONFIGURATION SECTION.
----►SOURCE-COMPUTER.              COPY   SRCCOM.
----►OBJECT-COMPUTER.              COPY   OBJCOM.
        DATA DIVISION.
        PROCEDURE DIVISION.
        0100-START.
            STOP RUN.
```

Compiling this program will reveal whether SRCCOM and OBJCOM are copyable and syntactically correct.

Continuation of the first stage entails supplying COPY statements to the skeleton program as additional entries are cataloged in the source library. At the completion of stage one, the skeleton program contains COPY statements for every data description cataloged in the source library pertaining to the specific application under construction. Coding errors are eliminated from the record descriptions by compiling the skeleton program and by removing any error diagnostics that are revealed.

Second Stage. The next step is to augment the procedure division with a standard structure that performs major procedures. This stage will give rise to program modules in which specific functions are implemented at predictable paragraphs. Revision to data descriptions are expected to be required; these changes will be recorded in the specific entries within the source library that are affected. A major advantage of using the COPY statement is that maintenance is localized in the source library, and the definitions are automatically available upon recompilation of those programs that exercise the COPY statement. Even such environmental changes as an upgrade of the computer mainframe can be accommodated simply by altering the source and object computer entries in the

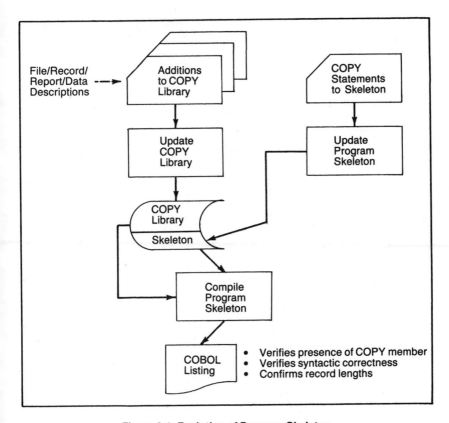

Figure 9-1. Evolution of Program Skeleton

library members SRCCOM and OBJCOM and by recompiling the source programs that copy these members. The need for software that identifies where specific library members are used is discussed later in this chapter. At the completion of stage two, the skeleton program would resemble the program shown in Figure 9-2.

Third Stage. The fully evolved program skeleton is now cloned as many times as there are modules to be produced for the entire application. Figure 9-3 illustrates this process. Each reproduction of the program skeleton is identical to the original except that the member name is that of the specific module to be developed. Although no fully implemented individual module will require all of these copy statements, each clone contains every copy statement that is available to the application.

Fourth Stage. The first level of customization begins in the fourth stage. At this point, the application programmer should receive the module specifications. Each specification should be reviewed against the version of the program skeleton to be customized. All inapplicable copy statements should be deleted.

```
000100* IDENTIFICATION DIVISION
000200*
000300* A BRIEF NARRATIVE OVERVIEW OF THE FUNCTION PERFORMED
000400* BY MODULE IS ENTERED HERE AS A REPLACEMENT FOR
000500* THIS COMMENT
000600* IF THE MODULE IS A SUBPROGRAM REQUIRING A CALLING
000700* SEQUENCE AN ILLUSTRATION OF THE CALL STATEMENT TO
000800* INVOKE THE MODULE IS SUPPLIED AS A COMMENT.
000900/
001000* PROGRAM-ID                SKELETON-PROGRAM
001100*
001200* THE ACTUAL PROGRAM-NAME INDICATED BY THE MODULE
001300* SPECIFICATION REPLACES THE OPERAND,
          'SKELETON-PROGRAM',
001400* AND THIS COMMENT IS THEN DELETED
001500*
001600* DATE-COMPILED             TODAY
001700* AUTHOR                    AUTHOR-NAME
001800*
001900* INSPECTED BY              REVIEWER-NAME
002000*
002100* INSTALLATION              INSTALLATION-NAME
002200/
002300*
002400* DATE-WRITTEN              DATE-WHEN-CODING-STARTED
002500* DATE-REVISED              DATE-OF-REVISION
002600* PROGRAM-STATUS            U
002700*   U - UNMODIFIED SKELETON
002800*   C - CODED                 M - MODIFIED SKELETON
002900*   P - PRODUCTION            T - TESTED
003000/                             R - UNDER REVISION
003100*
003200*
003300* ENVIRONMENT DIVISION
003400*
003500* CONFIGURATION SECTION
003600*
003700* SOURCE-COMPUTER           COPY SRCCOM
003800* OBJECT-COMPUTER           COPY OBJCOM
003900/
004000* INPUT-OUTPUT SECTION
004100*
004200* FILE-CONTROL.
004300*
004400*   SELECT       F1-filename-FILE      COPY select-1
004500*   SELECT       F2-filename-FILE      COPY select-2
004600/
004700*
004800* DATA DIVISION
004900*
005000* FILE SECTION
005100*
005200* FD  F1-filename-FILE
005300* 01  F1-filename-RECORD          COPY fld-1
                                        COPY record-1
005400/
005500* FD  F2-filename-FILE            COPY fld-2
005600* 01  F2-filename-RECORD          COPY record-2
005700/
005800*
005900* WORKING-STORAGE SECTION
006000/
006100* 01  W1-filename-RECORD          COPY record-1
006200*
006300* 01  W2-filename-RECORD          COPY record-2


006400* 01  W21-SWITCHES
006500*     03             W21-1-ON               PIC X  VALUE '1'
006600*     03             W21-2-OFF              PIC X  VALUE ZERO
006700*     03      88     W21-3-END-OF-FILE      PIC X  VALUE ZERO
006800*             88     CW21-3-1-MORE-DATA            VALUE '1'
006900*                    CW21-3-1-MORE-DATA
007000/                    CW21-3-2-NO-MORE-DATA
010000*
010100* PROCEDURE DIVISION
010200*
010300* 01-MAIN                                   SECTION
010400*
010500*
010600* 0100-START-OF-PROGRAM
010700*     PERFORM     7000-HOUSEKEEPING
010800*     PERFORM     0200-INPUT
010900*     IF          CW21-3-1-MORE-DATA
011000*        PERFORM     0300-INITIALIZE
011100*        PERFORM     0400-PROCESS
011200*        UNTIL       CW21-3-2-NO-MORE-DATA
011300*     PERFORM     8000-END-OF-JOB
011400*     STOP RUN
011500*
020000* 02-INPUT                                  SECTION
020100*
020200* 0200-INPUT
020300*     READ     input-file-name   INTO work-area   AT END
020400*        MOVE     W21-1-ON       TO  W21-3-END-OF-FILE
020500*
030000* 03-INITIALIZE                             SECTION
030100*
030200* 0300-INITIALIZE
030300*        ◄◄interpolate detail coding here
030400*
040000* 04-PROCESS                                SECTION
040100*
040200* 0400-PROCESS
040300*        ◄◄interpolate detail coding here
040400*
040500*     PERFORM     0200-INPUT
040600*
070000* 70-HOUSEKEEPING                           SECTION
070100*
070200* 7000-HOUSEKEEPING
070300*        ◄◄interpolate detail coding here
070400*
070500*
080000* 80-END-OF-JOB                             SECTION
080100*
080200* 8000-END-OF-JOB
080300*        ◄◄interpolate detail coding here
080400*
080500*
090000*
090100*                    END OF PROGRAM
090200*
090300*
```

Figure 9-2. Illustration of (COBOL) Programming Standards

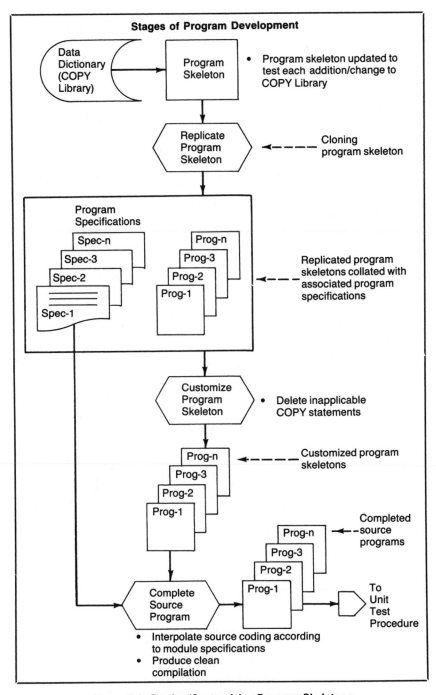

Figure 9-3. Cloning/Customizing Program Skeletons

In addition, the programmer should add commentary to the identification division that explains the function that the fully implemented module is to accomplish. The pared-down skeleton program should then be recompiled to ensure that it is free of error diagnostics. If the programmer has inadvertently deleted too many statements or otherwise clobbered his version of the skeleton, it is a simple matter to regenerate his starting point; in other words, stage three should be repeated. For any given module, a programmer should be able to complete the fourth stage in one day (assuming three test turnarounds).

Fifth Stage. The details of the module specifications are now implemented by the programmer making interpolations at the places indicated in the program skeleton (see Figure 9-3). Essentially, this is the point at which the programmer translates the analyst's pseudocode into compiler-intelligible code. Again, the module is compiled. When error free, the module is available for unit testing. This stage should be reached in approximately three days.

Sixth Stage. The completed module is tested using either a driver program (itself devised from an all-purpose test-driver skeleton program) or a partially completed version of the run unit where the top-level modules have already been customized (see Figure 9-4).

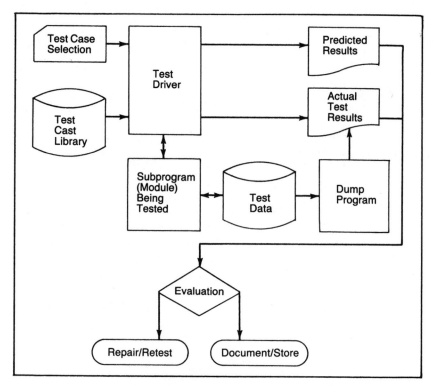

Figure 9-4. Use of Module Test Driver

Seventh Stage. When all modules comprising the run unit have been independently tested (stage six), they are fully integrated and the run unit is tested under conditions that simulate the actual production operation.

ADVANTAGES OF THE SKELETON PROGRAM METHOD

There are a number of reasons that building application modules from a common program skeleton that resides in a source statement library is desirable. These reasons are discussed in the following sections.

Custody. A problem that often besets the implementation of large computer-based applications is that of locating all code. When programmers are permitted to develop their own work individually, simply finding all the source programs is sometimes difficult. Having a disgruntled programmer quit and abscond with the only working version of a key source program is not unusual. Starting with all programs already recorded in a source library and customized therein ensures effective custody over all code (assuming that the library is regularly backed up for offline storage).

Illustration and Enforcement of Standards. Nearly every DP organization possesses and promulgates programming standards. These standards are often handsomely printed, bound in manuals, and conspicuously displayed. Typically, however, the standards are honored only in these manuals and are not observed in the working program code where they should be embedded.

Programmers are not always to blame for this. For one thing, standards are often not self-explanatory; they must be illustrated to be understood. Occasionally programmers are unaware that there are programming standards that they are expected to follow. Standards not applied in existing code are useless. The skeleton program provides working code built according to standards. The programmer is faced with prewritten code and the task of customizing that code according to standards already evident in the skeleton.

Uniformity. Managers must have the flexibility to reassign programmers in order to match their skills to the type and difficulty of the programming involved in particular modules. To achieve this flexibility, it is essential that all modules share a common architecture. The skeleton program ensures that all modules call identical functions by the same names. Consequently, a programmer need not be concerned with the idiosyncrasies of another programmer working on the same project. Data names and procedure names retain identical spelling and relative placement wherever they are specified. This facilitates the reassignment of work.

Control over Progress. Short-range customizing tasks provide a concrete basis for evaluating programmer skills. Progress is controlled effectively only when there are frequent checkpoints at which binary determinations (i.e., tasks are either completed or not) are made. Tasks are not considered in terms of percent completed; rather, only two percentages are reportable—100 percent or

0 percent. A 10-module program, for example, is 70 percent complete only when seven of the modules are 100 percent complete. Because modules are to be kept small (no more than 100 lines of procedural code), no module should require more than five working days to customize and unit test.

Visibility. The sight of a programmer hunched over a coding sheet or working at a screen reveals nothing about his progress or the quality of his work. Is he on the second of three pages or the second of three hundred? Until the program is unit tested, the quality of the code and its relevance to the program specification are not easily observed. The source-library discipline requires that the code be deposited in the library daily. This makes it easy to subject the programs to automated review.

The Copycall Procedure (see Figure 9-5) shows a utility that was devised in order to obtain reports on the status of modules in the source library and their interfaces. With such a utility, the project manager can obtain a daily census of modules and lines of code (See Figure 9-6). Furthermore, when any copyable entry is subject to change, the impact can be readily assessed by

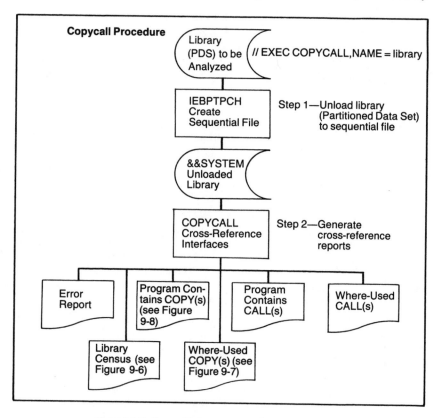

Figure 9-5. Cross-Referencing System Interfaces

```
OBJECT VERSION      13.45.37    MAR 13, 1979   CALL/COPY
RUN TIME/DATE       13 47 37    03/13/79       INPUT REPORT
                                               AY99300.DS.SOURCE3  (C)

       (A)                                                  (B)

 1. COPYCALL  ...............................................  697
 2. DATEWORK  ...............................................   14
 3. DEBUGCOM  ...............................................    5
 4. DEBUGGER  ...............................................   23
 5. DRIVER .................................................   95
 6. FD000001  ...............................................   10
 7. F0000001  ...............................................    5
 8. F0000002  ...............................................    5
 9. INFILFD  ................................................    6
10. INSEL  ..................................................    5
11. LIBMAINT  ...............................................  326
12. MOCKUP  .................................................   29
13. MOCKUP1  ................................................  191
14. OBJCOM  .................................................    5
15. OUTFILFD  ...............................................    7
16. OUTSEL  .................................................    5
17. PRINT01  ................................................  191
18. RD000000  ...............................................   59
19. RD000001  ...............................................   39
20. RD000003  ...............................................   37
21. RULER  ..................................................   37
22. RULER1  .................................................  297
23. SD000003  ...............................................   17
24. SKELETON  ...............................................  130
25. SORTSEL  ................................................    5
26. SQUAROOT  ...............................................  269
27. SRCCOM  .................................................    5
28. S0000003  ...............................................    5
29. TOGREGRY  ...............................................  129
30. TOJULIAN  ...............................................  112
                                                            =====
RECORDS SORTED ...... 142                              2.760  (D)
```

Legend:

A   Name of module or copyable component (library member)

B   Number of statements (coded lines) within library member

C   Name of library being cross-referenced

D   Total number of lines of code within library

Figure 9-6. Example of Library Census Report

reviewing the Where-Used Report (see Figure 9-7). Modules that have not been customized will exhibit profiles identical to that of the program skeleton. (For an example of the Program-Contains Report, see Figure 9-8.)

Reduction of Cost. The preceding advantages are all significant primarily because of their effect on the bottom line; they result in better-built applications constructed and maintained at lower cost. The benefit of using program skeletons as building blocks of a system is that one can treat a defective module like a burned-out light bulb. Rather than fix the module, one can replace it. Traditional systems generally are repaired not by replacing a bulb but by rewiring the building. Maintenance often consumes more than 60 percent of the programming budget because systems that were defective throughout the development stage are maintained. Programmers often solve a problem in one part of the

OBJECT VERSION 13 45 37   MAR 13, 1979   XREF /COPY STATEMENTS   PAGE 1
RUN TIME/DATE 13 47 37   03/13/79   AY99300.DS SOURCE3

COPYNAME	CONTAINED BY THESE MODULES						
DATEWORK	TOGREGRY-000073	TOJULIAN-000068					
DEBUGCOM	MOCKUP1--000025	RULER1--000026	SKELETON-000024	TOGREGRY-000023	TOJULIAN-000023		
DEBUGGER	SKELETON-000069						
E 0000001	COPYCALL-000080						
E 0000001	COPYCALL-000067						
E 0000002	COPYCALL-000068						
IMFILFD	MOCKUP1--000045	MOCKUP1--000046	RULER1--000048	RULER1--000049	SKELETON-000040		
IMSEL	MOCKUP1--000032	MOCKUP1--000035	RULER1--000035	RULER1--000038	SKELETON-000031		
MOCKUP	MOCKUP1--000088						
OBJCOM	COPYCALL-000057	DRIVER--000020	LIBMAINT-000017	MOCKUP1--000026	RULER1--000029	SKELETON-000025	TOGREGRY-00000
OBJCOM	TOJULIAN-000024						
OUTFILFD	MOCKUP1--000048	RULER1--000051	SKELETON-000042				
OUTSEL	MOCKUP1--000036	RULER1--000039	SKELETON-000033				
PRINT01	SKELETON-000062						
RD000000	COPYCALL-000248	COPYCALL-000250					
RD000001	COPYCALL-000270	COPYCALL-000272					
RD000003	COPYCALL-000282	COPYCALL-000284					
RULER	RULER1--000120						
SP000003	COPYCALL-000091						
SORTSEL	MOCKUP1--000037	RULER1--000040					
SRCCOM	COPYCALL-000055	DRIVER--000019	LIBMAINT-000016				
SR000003	COPYCALL-000070						

Note:
Each COPY member listed on the left is used by the source programs listed on the right.

Figure 9-7. Example of Where-Used COPY(s) Report

```
OBJECT VERSION   13.45.37   MAR 13, 1979   COPY STATEMENTS WITHIN MODULE                                    PAGE 1
RUN TIME/DATE    13.47.37   03/13/79       AY99300.DS.SOURCE3

MODULE         CONTAINS THESE MEMBERS
------         ----------------------

COPYCALL       F0000001-000080    F0000001-000067    F0000002-000068    OBJCOM---000057    RD000000-000248    RD000000-000250    RD000001-000270
COPYCALL       RD000001-000272    RD000003-000282    RD000003-000284    SD000003-000091    SRCCOM---000055    S0000003-000070
------
DRIVER         OBJCOM---000020    SRCCOM---000019
------
LIBMAINT       OBJCOM---000017    SRCCOM---000016
------
MOCKUP1        DEBUGCOM-000025    INFILFD-000045     INFILFD-000046     INSEL----000032    INSEL----000035    MOCKUP---000088    OBJCOM---000026
MOCKUP1        OUTFILFD-000048    OUTSEL---000036    SORTSEL-000037
------
RULER1         DEBUGCOM-000026    INFILFD-000048     INFILFD-000049     INSEL----000035    INSEL----000038    OBJCOM---000029    OUTFILFD-000051
RULER1         OUTSEL---000039    RULER----000120    SORTSEL-000040
------
SKELETON       DEBUGCOM-000024    DEBUGGER-000069    INFILFD-000040     INSEL----000031    OBJCOM---000025    OUTFILFD-000042    OUTSEL---000033
SKELETON       PRINT01-000062
------
TOGREGRY       DATEWORK-000073    DEBUGCOM-000023    OBJCOM---000023
TOJULIAN       DATEWORK-000068    DEBUGCOM-000023    OBJCOM---000023
------
```

Notes:
Each COBOL source module is shown in far-left column.
Copied library members and statment numbers of the COPY statements are
shouwn on the right

Figure 9-8. Example of Program Contains COPY(s) Report

system only to experience a negative side effect elsewhere. Furthermore, new programmers often spend weeks trying to understand the code they must maintain.

Program developers seldom consider the needs of the maintenance programmer. What the skeleton program method accomplishes is verifying that the development programmer *is* a maintenance programmer. Maintenance begins with the customization of the undifferentiated program skeleton. Some modules developed in this manner may even be reusable in other applications. How many installations have 10 or more date routines distributed in various applications? In fact, the calendar has probably been reinvented more often than the wheel.

CONCLUSION

Application programming can be approached as an assembly-line discipline. When selecting an application that has been designed but not yet specified, the methodology described in this chapter should be considered as follows:

- Define all data descriptions, and catalog the structures containing them in a source-program library.
- Evolve the program skeleton to exercise the COPY function to verify the presence and syntactic correctness of cataloged descriptions.
- Replicate the skeleton, using the planned names of each module to be developed.
- Build program specifications that list the COPY statements required for each module.
- Assign programmers to implement the customizing of the program skeletons by following the steps outlined in this chapter.

From this course of action will emerge an integrated, modular system that is readily maintainable and that has been produced on a timely and cost-beneficial basis.

10 Tools for Top-Down Testing

by Paul F. Barbuto, Jr.

INTRODUCTION

As the DP industry matures and society becomes more dependent on computers, spectacular failures of computer systems must be avoided. The concern for producing correct systems has, therefore, stimulated investigation of such techniques as top-down design and structured programming.

Top-down design and structured programming take a high-level functional requirement and decompose it into subgoals that, when achieved, enable the original requirement to be met. Testing provides a method for assessing whether functional requirements are being fulfilled and whether there are errors in the implementation of the design. This, however, is not quite enough to ensure that a system or program is "correct." For correctness, a system or program must, in addition, not go haywire when confronted with incorrect input data. A good testing program, therefore, is designed to search out boundary conditions (i.e., those between correct and out-of-range data) and generate multiple errors to test program reaction to unusual conditions. In addition, a good testing program ensures execution of all of the code.

TYPES OF TESTING

There are two ways to look at the testing process. The black-box approach evaluates a program based on whether it operates in the manner described in the specification. The white-box approach looks inside the program and analyzes the code in an attempt to demonstrate the functions of the software and understand their relationships. This type of testing then attempts to use the knowledge gained from the analysis to increase the thoroughness and variety of the test data.

Black-box testing depends on the correctness of the functional specification. This is both a blessing and a curse: a blessing in that it underscores the need for good documentation; a curse in that if the documentation is poor, nonexistent, or late, the planning of the testing is delayed and therefore can be rushed or inadequate.

In addition to these testing operating modes, there are three dynamic testing strategies from which to choose—bottom up, top down, and mixed.

Bottom-Up Testing. Bottom-up testing is a stepped process in which individual modules are tested first, subsystems (combinations of modules) are tested next, and system integration testing is performed when the other two steps have been completed successfully. It should be noted that this process can make for extremely complex integration testing and requires a test harness for each module and subsystem.

Top-Down Testing. Top-down testing, which assumes a hierarchical structure, first tests the main program with one or two immediately subordinate subroutines. Then, using the just-tested modules as a test harness, subordinate subroutine levels are tested one at a time. This process continues until all subroutines have been tested. Because this type of testing proceeds in the opposite direction from that of bottom-up testing, test stubs are required, rather than test harnesses. It should be noted, however, that whereas test harnesses (drivers) are usually discarded after use, test stubs can often be expanded into the modules that they are written to replace.

Top-down testing is the third link in the chain that also consists of top-down design and structured programming. With it, testing can begin earlier in the development process and be distributed, to some degree, throughout the life cycle. When the test designer is preparing tests sequentially as new modules are added to the program, the ramifications of adding a particular module of code can be seen. Furthermore, the number of test cases that must be added to exercise the new code is minimal.

AN EXAMPLE OF TOP-DOWN TESTING

Let us use the easy-to-understand example of designing, coding, and testing a card-to-print program using top-down methods. The initial goal, providing a card-to-print program, is illustrated in Figure 10-1. This function forms the top level of the hierarchy that will be constructed as the program function is decomposed. In this example, we name the top-level routine CRDPRNT.

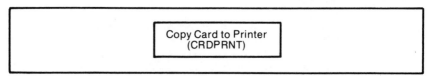

Figure 10-1. Sample Top-Down Design—Main Program Goal

If top-down implementation and testing are to progress as they should, the next step is to generate proper JCL for the ''program'' and compile and execute it with just the DECLARE statement for the variable buffer in it. When this version of the program is working (and it should be, quickly), one is ready to refine (or decompose) the top-level function. To do a card-to-print, the following functions must be performed: open the files, process the records, close the files, and report the record counts. These subgoals represent the second level of the hierarchy; they become four subroutines that are called by the main logic path, CRDPRNT. For purposes of this example, these routines are named

OPENFILS, PRCSRCRD, CLOSFILS, and RPRTCNTS, respectively (see Figure 10-2). When first generated, the new routines need only contain comments indicating their intended functions.

When this version of the program is working, one would add appropriate JCL and actually open and close the input and output files (without actually reading or writing them).

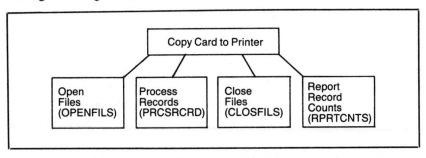

Figure 10-2. Sample Top-Down Design—First Level of Decomposition

The next level of the hierarchy includes decomposition of the PRCSRCRD routine. Getting a record (GETRCRD) and printing a record (PRNTRCRD) are the two functions that comprise the process record function; the design to this point is shown in Figure 10-3. Note that an automatic transfer at end-of-file makes this routine into a DO WHILE loop. As such, the READ in GETRCRD must be included or the DO WHILE loop will never be satisfied. At this point, the program can be executed with a null input file (and later with real input data).

The last step would be to actually write the code that puts the record out (in PRNTRCRD) and also the routine that increments the output record counter each time a record is written, and then test the entire program.

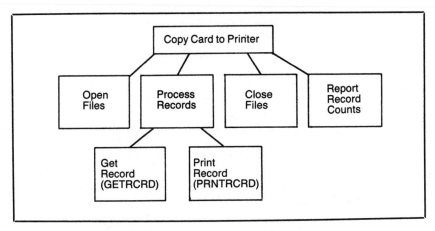

Figure 10-3. Further Decomposition of the Top-Down Design Example

The Benefits of Top-Down Testing

Top-down testing is beneficial to both management and the programming staff. Because it is more timely and manageable, both cost savings and a more reliable product are likely to result.

Concurrent top-down design, coding, and testing begin to produce parts of the final product early in the production cycle. This is achieved without risking an early start to implementation without proper analysis. It gives all concerned a real object to relate to, which can lead to higher morale and less tension between the planners and the doers.

The constant feedback to the analyst provided by top-down testing points to problem areas long before the system is complete. This early warning is useful because it is harder to determine what caused a bug in a processing routine if the first time it is apparent is during a test of the complete program.

With top-down testing, it is often possible to show the results of the last test to the end user, with an explanation such as, "At this time, the program can read all of the proposed input record types, and it can locate absurd values in input cards." This makes it possible to enlist the user's assistance and capitalize on his knowledge of the application.

When testing is integrated with development, some of the usual testing effort devoted to understanding the program is unnecessary. Since testing is spread over the entire project, demands for huge blocks of computer time for testing are avoided near project completion. In general, this tends to level the computer demands of the project over the life of the project—with respect to testing as well as implementation.

It is the nature of top-down design that as one goes down the hierarchy, the scope of a particular goal becomes smaller and the tasks needed to accomplish it more specific. Thus, as one designs and programs from the top down, a clearer and clearer opinion of what is necessary to complete the program is developed.

The part of the program that is written first is the main decision logic controller. This is important and useful since it is tested and retested each time new code is added at a lower level. Thus, that which, if incorrect, could do the most damage and be hardest to debug receives the most testing under the top-down testing approach.

TOOLS FOR TOP-DOWN TESTING

Hardware costs are decreasing, hardware speed is increasing, and staff costs are increasing; a worthwhile management strategy, therefore, is to let the machine assist the programmer. One way to do this is to build generalized tools that collect data about programs that are being written and display it in such a way that programmers can evaluate the quality of the design, the programming, and the testing that are being done.

Such programmer aids can be used in a number of ways, including:
- As part of the program and design under construction
- As part of the translator program

- As part of a preprocessor
- As part of the operating system

Flow Trace

A flow trace attempts to capture the dynamic sequence of program activities over time by, in some fashion, recording milestones passed. This definition is vague because flow traces vary a great deal. Unfortunately, flow traces are not always easy to get or, just as bad, are not very meaningful.

One way of realizing meaningful flow traces is by interposing a preprocessor between the source program and the translator. A simple preprocessor (i.e., one that was written in half a day) takes properly coded FORTRAN comments (those with a "CT" in columns one and two) and makes WRITE statements out of them. The output of the preprocessor is sent through the compiler, and the program's flow is displayed "in your own words." With this sort of trace and the value of a few key variables available from the debug INIT option, a lot of testing can be accomplished.

To obtain a production version of the code, the source program can be recompiled without first passing it through the preprocessor and changing the debug packet into comment statements. A similar comment converter has been implemented for PL/1, using preprocessor procedures—one set of procedures for testing, the other set for production. Any language with a macro facility can be provided with this type of enhanced flow-trace facility.

Completeness of Testing Coverage

As mentioned in the opening sections of this chapter, another requirement of a good testing strategy is to verify that all parts of the program code have been executed. Although executing all parts of the program does not ensure that testing is complete, not going through each part at least once surely indicates failure to provide complete test data.

Probes to collect test coverage data can be inserted by a preprocessor, just as meaningful flow traces can. Alternatively, or better still, some form of summary statistics should be included. A competently written piece of software would usually include the number and types of records processed, the number and types of errors generated, the number of records read, and the number of records written.

When considering testing coverage, it may very well be necessary to keep the results of testing over multiple runs to provide the summary as described. This is because you cannot have both no input records and records displaying certain properties in the same run. Testing may have to be spread over different executions of the program.

Flow Groups

A flow group is a single-entry, single-exit block of code that contains no transfers. This concept is important when deciding where to place probes to capture flow information; flow data must only be captured once per flow group.

Sequences of Flow Groups. As was mentioned in the section on testing completeness, merely passing through each section of code is not necessarily indicative of a complete test. Going through all possible sequences of flow groups, however, is a better indication.

Probes to collect flow-group execution data are easily included in a program. The data can be recorded in an M × M matrix, where M is the number of flow groups. The matrix is initialized to zero the first time it is used. An entry is made in (i.e., one is added to) the matrix location associated with the appropriate row-column pair when a transition occurs between one flow group and another. The row number is determined by the "from" flow group. The column number is determined by the "to" flow group. Interpretively, nonzero rows are rows associated with flow groups from which transitions occur. Nonzero columns are columns associated with flow groups into which transitions occur.

Armed with sequential flow-group data, one must still decide whether these are the only possible transitions and whether a particular transition has been exercised for all possible reasons. For example, if a bug occurs only when two error transactions of a particular type occur in sequence, it might remain undetected if all possible sequences are not tested. Going from the flow group associated with a correct transaction to that of an incorrect transaction, to another error, to a correct transaction will represent adequate testing only if there is only one possible error. Because it is always possible that there are many errors, the entire flow-group matrix must be filled in in order to be certain that all such "combination" errors have been detected.

If it is necessary to summarize over different runs, the matrix must be written out and read in at the beginning of the next run, unless matrices are to be preserved separately for each run and externally combined. This is probably the preferred approach in that the effect of each batch of test data can be inspected individually.

Module Structure Hierarchy

Another useful program that can assist in visualizing the top-down structure of a program is a program that traces through all macro expansions and text inclusions and displays the implied structure. Such a program aids in keeping documentation up-to-date, since it is easier to command the machine to redraw a hierarchy chart than to require a programmer or clerk to do the same task. It is also more cost-effective. Such a program, appropriately named Tree, was developed at the Multistate Patient Information System at the Rockland State Hospital in Orangeburg, New York. The program scans a PL/1 source-library partitioned data set containing a main routine and included members (CALLed subroutines). It then draws a tree, taking its text from the comments that would be generated into trace statements placed at the beginning and end of each module. Its structuring of the tree is based on the nesting of these beginning- and end-of-module indicators. This is possible since the structure of a tree can be represented as a series of parentheses; the tree representing the hierarchy of modules in the skeleton PL/1 program shown in Figure 10-3 is shown in

Figure 10-4. In programs where there are many common routines realized by subroutine calls, a display similar to that proposed for the module hierarchy is useful.

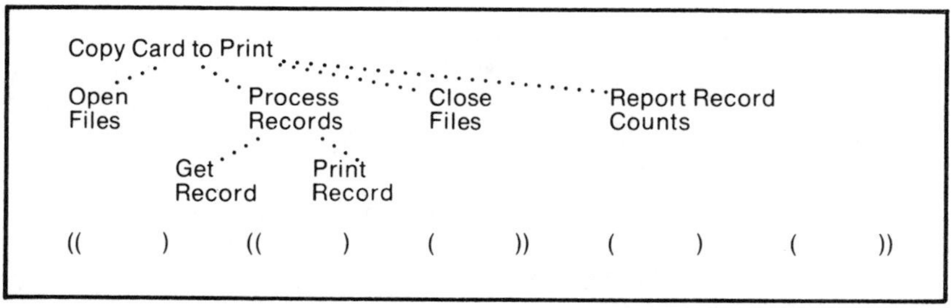

```
┌─────────────────────────────────────────────────────────────────────┐
│  Copy Card to Print                                                   │
│       · ·                                                             │
│   Open          · Process         Close       · · · ·Report Record    │
│   Files           Records         Files              Counts           │
│           · ·           ·                                             │
│       Get ·        Print                                              │
│       Record       Record                                             │
│                                                                       │
│   ((     )    ((     )     (     ))    (     )     (     ))           │
└─────────────────────────────────────────────────────────────────────┘
```

Figure 10-4. Module Structure Hierarchy Display

Automated Regression Testing

Once a program gets big enough to require extensive tests, the problem of generating adequate test data is only surpassed by the problem of reading test results. Harnessing the computer to read and evaluate its own test output can go a long way toward solving the latter problem.

One type of computer self-testing that can be built into systems that must be extremely reliable is to have the systems software execute problems with known solutions and check the results during idle moments. Any deviation from expected results indicates failure of some sort and is cause for alarm. Any program execution under test, with test data for which known, expected, or approved results are available, is called a regression test. If a regression test is run successfully, when a bug is fixed, one knows that additional bugs have not been (re)introduced into already-tested code, at least not within the coverage of the existing test data. This should be reassuring, since the test data was considered to have been adequate in the past or is at least the best currently available.

When top-down testing is being performed on a new system, regression testing is done as the system modules are being integrated. Regression testing attempts to ensure that the addition of a new module has not adversely affected the previously tested modules. As an example, consider a project where the primary goal is to rewrite an existing program to decrease execution time and produce a well-documented top-down version of the data base summary file generator. Regression testing could be accomplished in this case by comparing the output files generated by the old and new versions of the program with the standard IBM utility program IEBCOMPR. This would be done after blanking out those parts of the records in the files that one knows would be different, either because of known bugs in the old program or because parts of the program have not yet been implemented. Ultimately, the corrected parts would have to be verified manually, but the bulk of the comparison could be done by the computer. This technique enables one to test early program versions and get run timings as the development effort progresses.

String-Matching Problems. The problem of automatic output reading generally boils down to string-matching; the problem is threefold. The first difficulty is in selecting the string to be compared, which, depending on context, can be difficult. The second difficulty can arise in comparing the string. This is relatively easy to do unless a tolerance band is allowed. The third problem is that of resynchronization after a nonmatch, or because a fix or addition is generating new output. The most likely solution to such a resynchronization problem is the purposeful generation of milestones of some nature (e.g., beginning of transaction xxx).

Remember, a computer is better suited to read and check voluminous test results than is the average human; it is tireless and a stickler for detail. Solving these string-matching problems will probably result in an excellent return on the time and resources invested.

CONCLUSION

The use of the top-down method of testing with the associated tools described in this chapter can do the following:
* Provide a low-risk environment and increased programmer productivity
* Provide earlier feedback to systems analysts, designers, and users
* Shorten project test time and total development time
* Provide more accurate project completion data
* Result in more thoroughly tested control logic

Furthermore, developing the testing tools required to support top-down testing will constitute a relatively minor investment of programmer time and effort.

The challenge of the 1980s is to condition programmers to view testing in a positive light and to integrate top-down testing into the design development cycle. Making tools available to facilitate this integration will improve programmer productivity. Testing needs science, not art; tools, not techniques.

Bibliography

Barbuto, Paul and Geller, Joe. "Tools for Top-Down Testing." *Datamation*, Vol. 24, No. 10 (October 1978), 178-182.

Fairley, Richard E. "Tutorial: Static Analysis and Dynamic Testing of Computer Software." *Computer*, Vol. 11, No. 4 (April 1978), 14-23.

Hetzel, William C., ed. *Program Test Methods*. Englewood Cliffs NJ: Prentice-Hall Inc, 1973.

IBM OS PL/1 Optimizing Compiler General Information. GC33-001-2.

McGowan, Clement L., and Kelly, John R. *Top-Down Structured Programming Techniques*. New York: Petrocelli/Charter, 1975.

Rustin, Randall, ed. *Debugging Techniques in Large Systems*. Englewood Cliffs NJ: Prentice-Hall Inc, 1971.

Westley, Anne E., ed. *Infotech State of the Art Report, Software Testing, Volume 1: Analysis and Bibliography*. Maidenhead, England: Infotech International Limited, 1979. Contributions by Fairley, Howden, Clarke, Kundu, and the editor.

Yourdon, Edward. *Techniques of Program Structure and Design*. Englewood Cliffs NJ: Prentice-Hall Inc, 1975.

11 A Methodology for Program Maintenance

by David M. Clark

INTRODUCTION

The large, complex systems currently demanded by users require detailed knowledge of a given system in order to effect even the smallest change without disruption. The high turnover in many DP shops, however, combined with the need to rotate creative, easily bored people through various programming challenges often requires that programmers make changes to a program or system about which they know little.

Determining where and how to change an unfamiliar program under such circumstances can be a serious problem. This chapter addresses this topic and discusses program overviews, organization, and documentation as they relate to program maintenance. Techniques for quickly and efficiently finding the right code to change and ways of making future programs easy to maintain are presented.

THE CHANGE TASK OVERVIEW

Determining where to change or not change a program is one of the biggest problems maintenance programmers face; typically, they spend a great deal of time on frustrating, misdirected, expensive searches for the right code. It is a truism of programming that it takes more time to find where to change a program than it does to make the change. Consequently, the methodology discussed here emphasizes the proper preparation for making a change, rather than the change itself. It is easy to write a MOVE statement in COBOL; however, it is harder to know where to put that MOVE statement.

Importance of the Task

Management's first step in trying to control the maintenance effort should be to indicate to the maintenance programmers the importance and priority of each maintenance task. This step is important but often overlooked. Because maintenance is the frequent burden of those least qualified to perform it (trainees and programmers who are new to the shop), cost overruns often start with this first step. Management should pay careful attention to the cost:benefit ratio of each maintenance task in determining its importance in relation to the overall work load. It should be remembered, of course, that the additional expense incurred by using new or inexperienced programmers is a training cost that should be assumed by programming management. Thus, if the cost of changing a program exceeds the immediate benefit to be derived, management should determine whether the task should be given a lower priority, completed by someone more knowledgeable about the system, or perhaps not performed at all.

Available Resources

Determining and marshalling the resources available to the maintenance programmer should be performed early in the maintenance effort. To do this, management should ask the following questions:

- Are programmers who are knowledgeable about this system available to help the maintenance programmer? How much time can they afford to spend in the change task? Although knowledgeable, experienced programmers should always be made available to maintenance personnel, the amount of time actually spent assisting in the change will vary greatly, depending primarily on the skills and background of the maintenance programmer.
- Has the maintenance programmer been assigned permanent responsibility for maintaining this program? If so, allowing the maintenance programmer extra time to become familiar with the entire program will pay dividends later in the form of faster response to critical system crashes or top-priority "hot" changes.
- How much time is available for testing? If a programmer can complete only one or two test runs a day, extra emphasis must be placed on analyzing and desk-checking the required changes.
- How difficult is it to test the changes? Can the maintenance programmer try out several changes quickly and easily, or should dry runs and testing models be relied on? Failure to determine the optimum testing/desk-checking ratio of a maintenance effort is another reason for time and cost overruns.

Change Instructions

Careful attention to change instructions is another important part of getting an overview of the maintenance task. Change instructions should always be in writing; unwritten instructions invite problems, including:

- Problems in determining why the change was made—after it causes unpredictable or unforeseen results.
- Problems in determining who asked for the change—Did the person have the authority (especially if he or she was not the sole user of the program's output)?
- Problems in determining the scope of the change—Why were only certain programs or certain sections of a program changed?

In addition to serving as a record of the change, written instructions often force the user to be more explicit and thorough in determining what should be changed. Written instructions, however, may still not be enough, and management should urge maintenance programmers to speak directly with the user who first requested the change. The maintenance programmer can then compare the written instructions with the user's interpretation of them. (It is worth noting that most user-related DP problems are communications rather than technical problems.)

A simple example illustrates this written versus oral communication process. A user requested two changes to a program that produced a budget report very similar to a more frequently used actual expense report. Recent changes had been made to the expense program, and in discussing the changes with the user, the maintenance programmer discovered that the user really wanted the two report formats to correspond exactly. Instead of having to hunt and peck to make the requested changes, the programmer simply inserted in the first program all recent changes made to the second program. The task became logically easier to accomplish since the programmer did not have to determine where the two programs differed; it took only slightly longer to do, and the user was satisfied.

THE PROGRAM OVERVIEW

An overview of the program or programs to be changed is as important as an overview of the change task. The length of time spent on this overview will, of course, depend upon the importance assigned to the task.

Program Purpose and Type

This overview should attempt to determine the program purpose and type by addressing the following questions:

- What is the basic purpose of this program? Is it a report generator, a file update, or an edit/update?
- What is the primary output of the program? If the result or objective of the program is known, it is easier to understand intermediate calculations or processing.
- What is the basic framework of the program? How are loops handled? What type of organization does the program have—formally structured, loosely structured (GO TOs allowed, within limits), or waterfall (GO TOs cascading down through the program)?
- What was the style of the programmer who originally wrote the program? Most programmers have styles of coding as individual, and sometimes as hard to comprehend, as their handwriting. Understanding how loops are handled in a simple section of code will probably help the programmer understand how loops are coded in a more difficult section. A programmer's style is revealed in such things as how data names are formed, how IF conditions are handled (positive or negative logic), and so on.

Answering these questions will help the programmer make intelligent guesses about what the program will do in the section requiring change. The programmer will thus be able to decide more quickly, with more assurance, what will happen if the program control statements (and hence program logic) are changed.

Program Control Structure

Getting an overview is usually easier with a program that has some structure (i.e., it falls somewhere between modularized and formally structured). In such a program, the major sections are identified in some sort of mainline or high-level processing module, and the major processing loops are usually isolated and thus easily identified. The section that needs to be changed can therefore be located far more quickly and easily than in an unstructured program. This is frequently given as a major justification for writing structured code.

Getting an overview of an unstructured program is more difficult. It may, in fact, be impossible in a program with countless hard-to-follow GO TOs, in which case the programmer may be forced to start the overview at the beginning, with the first procedural statement, and follow each one sequentially. A more rational and efficient method is first to stake out the major boundaries of program logic in order to break the program down into its identifiable sections (mainline code, initialization routines, and the like). This process, which makes an unstructured program emulate a structured one, is necessary to determine into which section the change will fall.

The easiest way to do this is to look for the major processing loops in a program, since they serve as the boundaries, or "fence posts," of logic. Almost every program has them, even if implied (PERFORM UNTIL or DO WHILE). The main loops are usually marked, especially in an unstructured program, by some type of input statement, usually a read, and a program control statement such as GO TO. Underlining these statements on the source listing can be helpful. Particular attention should be paid to unconditional branches, looking, for example, for GO TOs before paragraph or section names in COBOL—especially GO TOs that loop back to the main input paragraph.

Picking out the major loops in an unfamiliar program has a tremendous psychological advantage also: It reassures the programmer that there is, in fact, some way to understand and therefore change a complex program. This advantage is not to be taken lightly, since frustration over a seemingly incomprehensible program frequently causes programmers to make careless, stab-in-the-dark changes. These are the changes that return to haunt their successors in the form of system crashes, missing input, and the like. From this comes the infamous vicious circle in which programmers do not have enough time to write correct, easy-to-maintain programs because they are too busy putting out the fires of someone's previous mistakes.

Extraneous Sections

Ignoring the parts of the program that will not be affected by the change is one of the most important—yet most difficult—steps in maintenance programming; however, it is this step that causes programmers so much trouble. Some general guidelines can be given as to which areas of a program can be ignored, at least on the first pass. Initialization sections, for example, are usually important only later, when the programmer needs to know when and where a key data field is first accessed. Sections that build tables internally are important only when changing the layout of those tables; otherwise, the programmer can concentrate on what is done after data is stored on the tables. In a file update program, the key matching logic can be ignored if the change affects only the output on one of those files.

DETERMINING WHERE TO MAKE THE CHANGE

Performing the steps discussed simplifies the task of weeding out inapplicable parts of the program. Keeping an overview of the program in mind and knowing the style of the original programmer, the maintenance programmer can determine where the mainline section of the program falls, where initialization is performed, when the program is likely to loop—and why—and, in general, focus on the specific section to be changed. The programmer's familiarity with the change instructions may then allow the change to be made directly, without any further analysis.

If the program to be changed is particularly incomprehensible or if the programmer has been unable to get an overview, an alternative strategy for determining where to make the change may be necessary. This alternative strategy focuses on the specific data element to be changed. If the programmer knows the program data name for that data element, he or she can find out where the element is accessed in the program cross-reference dictionary. If the programmer does not know the exact name of a data element, the cross-reference dictionary can be searched for a name suggesting that data element or data function. If the data segment (record) is to be changed but the programmer does not know where to find the code that accesses that data segment, he or she can look for the occurrences of one of the fields in that record in the cross-reference dictionary. An analogy can be drawn to a too-large or confusing pattern in a piece of fabric; following a certain strand of cloth may help decipher the pattern.

A data movement chart (see Figure 11-1) may help. Starting at the right-hand side of a paper, a box should be drawn containing the last output field name. The lines in the program in which that field appears should be indicated below the box. One checks each occurrence of the field, crossing out superfluous accesses and concentrating on the lines in which the field is created or otherwise manipulated. Fields that provide data for that output field are drawn to the left of the field, in their own boxes, with arrows connecting the two boxes, showing the direction of the data movement. The statements that modify or create the data can be written above those arrows. This process of working

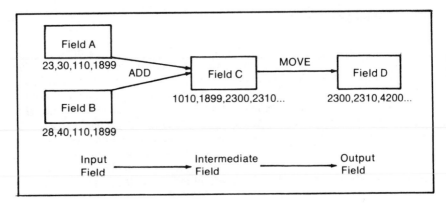

Figure 11-1. Data Movement Chart

backward through each field is continued until the original source of the data, or the field that needs to be changed, is encountered The data movement chart can then be filed with the change instructions for subsequent use by other maintenance programmers.

Data movement can also be traced through procedural names. The paragraph or section that needs to be changed would become the last output box, and all paragraphs or sections that perform or branch to that section would become the intermediate boxes to be traced in this manner

MAKING THE CHANGE

Although maintenance programmers should not go overboard with maintenance changes, they should not be afraid to make a change. Most novice maintenance programmers, however, go through an unfortunate cycle in making program changes. They start out eager to set things straight and become overanxious about their deadlines and work load. (This anxiety underscores the importance of assigning priorities.) As a result, the programmers often make more changes than necessary, learning very soon that changing code because it is not sufficiently elegant can lead to sudden and disastrous results. Feeling foolish about their programming idealism, they overreact, vowing to change only the bare minimum of code in all future maintenance tasks.

Management should stress to the maintenance programmers that this "once burned, twice shy" philosophy is not necessarily effective programming, although it neatly fits in with the novice's defense mechanism. People write code, and people can change code. Changes can and should be made to poorly written or incomprehensible programs to make them easier to follow and thus to change.

Conversely, management should also stress the value of using code that one is reasonably confident already works. Not all existing code works, to be sure, but it must be given the benefit of the doubt if changes are to be made in a reasonable amount of time. Similar routines in existing programs can often be copied or modified into the program to be changed. Establishing libraries or directories of commonly used routines can be one of management's greatest services for its maintenance programmers.

This is also a good time for a maintenance programmer, with the program logic still fresh in his or her mind, to consider what other changes the user might want in the near future. Management, by apprising the programmers of long-term user objectives and plans as well as organizational considerations, can aid in this process.

MAKING FUTURE CHANGES EASIER

After a stint doing maintenance, most programmers appreciate the difficulties involved in changing obscure, hard-to-follow code. This may be why some companies start their trainees in maintenance programming.

Documenting the Change

One of the best ways to ensure that future changes are easier to make is to document what has been learned about the program logic (in addition to documenting the changes currently being made). For example, a few words inserted directly into the code about what a switch does, where it is initialized, under what conditions this paragraph is performed, and so on can help subsequent programmers tremendously. In the absence of management directives to perform this type of documentation (a lack that is hard to understand, given the amount of time and money spent doing maintenance tasks), programmers who do perform it sometimes start a trend toward greater documentation in their shops. This trend has even spread to those who insisted they would not, or could not, document. It is interesting to watch these programmers making changes to an unfamiliar program. When scanning a page of code, their eyes usually jump immediately to any documentation, even if the documentation is irrelevant or out of date. Once in place, program documentation is hard to ignore.

The pros and cons of documentation, and how to document effectively, lie outside the scope of this chapter. The question most frequently asked when a program has problems is: Has it been changed lately? The following simple guidelines should prove helpful in answering this question:

- Documentation should be done at the lowest level possible in the system hierarchy, which is usually where the changes to the program were made. Although separate documentation folders or program/system narratives are helpful (and important), they are too far removed from the level of the system that changes most frequently. Most programmers go to the code first when they need to change a program; the documentation should be put there.
- Some reference to the task or change instructions should be put in the code. This enables subsequent programmers to spot the changed code quickly. For example, the word "TASK" followed by a 4-position task number could be inserted in columns 73 to 80 of COBOL source programs. If a programmer wanted additional information, he or she

could pull the file on that task (if easily retrievable) to gather such additional information as the original user change request or notes made during the change.

- The changes to the program should be filed with the program source listing. This supplements the previous suggestion and provides a ready reference to the changes. For example, a copy of the permanent program changes could be filed in front of the COBOL source listings, allowing programmers to tell instantly whether the program has been changed recently.

Structured Retrofit

One concept that can aid program maintainability is that of structured retrofit [1], which is basically the process of redesigning existing programs to conform to the latest structured programming techniques. (This effort would, of course, not be required if a system redesign were being considered.) A project team consisting of a chief programmer, programmer analysts, and supporting personnel reviews existing programs to determine which need improvement most. These programs are then changed, using certain criteria that primarily emphasize clarity of logic flow, I/O standardization, and readability; they are not, however, changed to correct any revealed errors, bugs, or user requests.

The idea of systematically revamping and retrofitting all programs not meeting current standards is appealing and could probably be cost-justified following sufficient research into a shop's current maintenance costs. It may not be practical, however, for a maintenance programmer to wait for such a retrofit to take place, given the current backlog, in most DP organizations, of higher-priority projects with more user appeal.

There may be cases, of course, where a program is so incomprehensible that it may have to undergo redesign and reorganization before any maintenance can be done. In such cases, it may even be necessary to create a "shadow program." The shadow program is used only for maintenance efforts and contains the same code as the original program (identifiable dead code is removed) but in a rearranged sequence that is as straight line and as straightforward as possible. GO TO statements are taken to code on the same source page, not buried in the program. Additional comments, source line numbers of such statements, and paragraph or section headings can be handwritten on a listing of this shadow program. The shadow program may not be syntactically or logically correct (it may not even compile successfully), but it is a clearer, easier-to-read map of the original program. This listing is filed with the original program so that future maintenance programmers can have it as a ready reference.

Increasing Program Maintainability

Although a large-scale reorganization or retrofit may be politically or organizationally unfeasible, increasing a program's readability (and therefore maintainability) is a sound concept that can be applied by maintenance programmers, one program at a time. Certain changes can be made to any program that will render future maintenance changes easier but that do not necessarily involve a complete retrofit or reorganization and the consequent risk of altering program logic or output. These changes, which make a program easier to read and comprehend, include indentation; the ample use of blank space; succinct, meaningful comments; and the use of mnemonic names.

Indentation. Indentation is a simple, frequently overlooked way to improve program readability. Its major value lies in drawing the maintenance programmer's attention to the chief divisions of program logic or data structure. Code that is indented to other code suggests visually that it is dependent on or inferior to the nonindented code. The programmer, therefore, must keep in mind only the nonindented code, rather than the entire block of code. For example, with the following code in COBOL:

```
IF FRACTION-INPUT NOT = SPACES
    PERFORM A020-FRACTION-DECIMAL-CONVERT.
```

The indentation of "PERFORM A020-FRACTION-DECIMAL-CONVERT" suggests to the programmer, even if he or she does not know the syntactical requirements of the IF statement, that the PERFORM phrase is somehow dependent on the IF phrase. Without indentation, this dependence would not be suggested:

```
IF FRACTION-INPUT NOT = SPACES
PERFORM A020-FRACTION-DECIMAL-CONVERT.
```

As a result, the programmer would have to work harder to spot the IF statement and know that the syntax of the COBOL IF statement requires a subsequent imperative statement. Such additional time and knowledge requirements ultimately add to the cost of maintenance.

Open Space. The ample but judicious use of open space in a program listing can also improve program readability and maintainability. Open space emphasizes and attracts—a device used successfully in advertising. The boldest, most direct message is a simple sentence or two surrounded by uncluttered space. In the same manner, textbook editors separate chapter headings from text by open space. In a program, open space should be used around procedure headings (paragraph or section names in COBOL) and major divisions of the programs as well as individual statements. For example:

```
A020-FRACTION-DECIMAL-CONVERT.
```

Asterisks are also frequently used to highlight statements:

```
* * * * * * * * * * * * * * * * * * * * * * * *
*
*    A020-FRACTION-DECIMAL-CONVERT.      *
*                                         *
* * * * * * * * * * * * * * * * * * * * * * * *
```

Another example illustrates the importance of free space and indentation:

```
IF INPUT = SPACES MOVE ERROR-MESSAGE
TO DISPLAY-MESSAGE STOP RUN ELSE
MOVE INPUT TO HOLD-AREA GO TO CONTINUE.
```

This code obscures the major procedural statement STOP RUN, buried in the middle.

Comments. The use of succinct explanatory comments is another important part of program maintainability. There has been much hand-wringing over the seeming inability of many programmers to document their programs with comments; however, as noted previously, program comments, once in place, are visually hard to ignore. Given this prominence and the realization that the programming function is basically a process of mentally translating from one language (e.g., COBOL, FORTRAN) to another (e.g., English, German) each time a program is read (maintained), the use of comments to explain program logic assumes added importance. Management should require a reasonable number of program comments from the maintenance programmers (four or five lines of comments for every page of text; more for complex code, less for straightforward code).

Mnemonic Names. The use of meaningful mnemonic data and procedure names helps speed maintenance efforts, primarily because a programmer who knows what a section of code does (because of its representative name) does not have to worry about exactly how it does it. (This is the cornerstone of the black-box theory of software engineering, which has been used by computer and systems software designers for years.) In the previous example (PERFORM A020-FRACTION-DECIMAL-CONVERT.), the reader can probably assume that A020-FRACTION-DECIMAL-CONVERT takes some input fraction and converts it to its equivalent decimal. How it accomplishes that task is not important, especially if the programmer knows that the code has been obtained from another program or a system library and has probably been debugged already. In fact, if the output of that section of code is irrelevant to the sections that need to be changed, the maintenance programmer can ignore the section completely, speeding comprehension of the program.

These techniques for improving program maintainability are not to be taken lightly. In one experiment [2], participants in a simulated maintenance situation obtained significant results in terms of productivity and accuracy when they used indentation, comments, and meaningful mnemonics. The use of mnemonics created productivity gains of 48 percent, and the use of comments fostered gains of from 34 to 69 percent. Thus, these simple techniques provided significant gains.

CONCLUSION

A significant reduction in maintenance programming costs is possible when a methodology for maintaining programs is followed. This methodology should emphasize programmer preparation, program and task overview, and change follow-through. Documentation, both before and after the change, is also important. Revising current or writing future programs to include indentation, free space, comments, and mnemonic names will help to reduce future maintenance programming costs.

References

1. Miller, J.C. "Structured Retrofit." *Techniques of Program and System Maintenance.* Edited by Girish Parikh. Lincoln NE: Ethnotech Inc, 1980.
2. Gilb, T. "Structured Program Coding: Does It Really Increase Program Maintainability?" *Techniques of Program and System Maintenance.* Edited by Girish Parikh. Lincoln NE: Ethnotech Inc, 1980.